KU-033-304

WILFRED GRENFELL

THE
ARCTIC
ADVENTURER

WILFRED GRENFELL

THE
ARCTIC
ADVENTURER

LINDA
FINLAYSON

CHRISTIAN FOCUS

© Copyright 2004 Linda Finlayson
ISBN 1-85792-929-2
Published in 2004
by
Christian Focus Publications,
Geanies House, Fearn,
Ross-shire, IV20 1TW,
Great Britain

Supplementary sections
© Copyright 2004
Christian Focus Publications

Cover design by Alister Macinnes
Cover illustration by Fred Apps
Map by Fred Apps

Printed and bound in Great Britain by
Cox and Wyman Ltd, Reading, Berkshire

All rights reserved.No part of this publication may
be reproduced, stored in a retrieval system, or
transmitted, in any form, by any means, electronic,
mechanical, photocopying, recording or otherwise
without the prior permission of the publisher or a
license permitting restricted copying. In the U.K.
such licenses are issued by the Copyright
Licensing Agency, 90 Tottenham Court Road,
London W1P 9HE.

For Sandy and Ian

Contents

THE ICE PAN
ADVENTURE

'Faster, Jack, faster!' Wilfred called to his jet black retriever, who ran beside his dog sledge team. Jack needed no reminder. He loved to go fast and urged the team forward by moving ahead of them. The team of seven dogs surged forward.

Wilfred loved to go fast too, and felt a thrill as the cold wind blew past his face. He was rushing to see a very sick boy in Brent Island, about 60 miles down the coast of Newfoundland. It was April 1908 and Wilfred, was a fully qualified doctor working in one of the harshest climates in the northern hemisphere. He had just finished preaching the Easter morning sermon in St. Anthony when the message about the sick boy arrived. A bad case of gangrene had developed in the boy's leg. He needed to see the doctor urgently.

Wilfred did not hesitate. He went home and changed into his old football gear and put on a warm jacket, cap and gloves. He also wore his hip high sealskin boots. He probably should have dressed more warmly, but it was April after all, and not as cold as the dead of winter. He strapped on his hunting knife, picked up his medical bag, and set off on his journey.

Although he was 43 years old, Wilfred was still muscular and trim and always ready for an adventure. He had learned how to use a dog team and sledge a few years ago so that he could travel up and down the coast in the winter. Many of his patients were in small villages perched on the shore. In summer he visited them by boat and in the winter with his dog team. He loved his hardy dogs: Jack, Moody, Spy, Watch, Doc, Brin, Jerry and Sue. Together they had learned how to give and receive orders and make the sledge race over the snow. And could they race! There was such freedom flying across the deep snow or ice that would slow a walking person to a crawl.

The day was clear, with a touch of spring in the air. That should have alerted Dr. Grenfell to notice that spring was in the air - and with spring came the thaw and melting ice, but he was too busy enjoying the ride. However, the next morning, after spending the night in a little hamlet by the bay, the weather turned wet and foggy. Wilfred hoped to shorten his travel time by going across Hare Bay, rather than the longer overland route. They started out well. The ice was firm and the dogs raced along. But soon instead of hard ice they hit slush, which meant a patch of ice was melting and could break apart at any moment. 'Come on Jack,' Wilfred called out. 'Faster!' But it did not matter. They were already too far from land to go back. Then the worst thing happened. Right in front of the dogs the ice cracked open.

'Stop! Jack, stop!' Even as Wilfred called out the words, Jack had reached the yawning black hole. There was no way they could stop on the slippery ice. Wilfred watched in horror

11

as Jack and then one by one the other dogs slid into the freezing water. Thinking quickly, Dr. Grenfell whipped out his hunting knife and slashed at the leather harnesses that joined the team to the sledge. If the sledge was still attached to the dogs when it went in the water it would drag them down to the depths. Fortunately the leather harnesses fell away and the sledge disappeared into the wet darkness. Wilfred saw all of this just before he too hit the frigid water.

It was so cold that for a moment Wilfred could not breathe. He worked to keep his head above the water. His water-logged coat was so heavy if he did not let it go he would drown. He struggled out of the coat and let it sink beneath him. Then he spotted a large pan of ice. It looked solid enough to hold them all.

'Jack!' he called as he swam over to the dogs. He grabbed Jack's collar. 'Lead the others to the ice.'

But Jack was cold and confused. Ice began to form on his fur as he struggled to keep his head above the water. He did not understand what his master wanted.

What could Wilfred do to get Jack to obey? Then a small chunk of ice brushed up against him in the water. Smiling, Wilfred reached out for it. There was one game Jack loved to play.

'Fetch, Jack!' Dr. Grenfell called, and threw the chunk on to the ice pan.

Now Jack knew what to do. Barking for the others to follow, he swam with all his might to fetch the chunk of ice. Wilfred helped push each of his dogs on to the ice pan. Then, last of all, he hauled himself up out of the water.

Dogs and man had escaped drowning. But now they had bigger problems. The wind was picking up. Wilfred looked around. To his horror he realized that they were on a large flat piece of ice that was floating out to sea. The shore of Hare Bay was receding and there was no one to see what was happening. To make matters worse, his wet clothing was beginning to freeze along with his hair and moustache. Wilfred's teeth were chattering from the cold. He would not survive very long if he did not find a way to get warm.

Somewhere in his struggles he had lost his cap and gloves, and his sealskin boots were full of icy water.

Dr. Grenfell looked at his beloved dogs. Their fur was frozen and they were huddling together to try to find some warmth. Spy was whining a little. Wilfred touched his hunting knife and wished he did not know what he had to do. But there was no choice otherwise they would all die very soon.

Wilfred called Spy, a wiry powerful black and white dog, to him and held him close. 'Sorry, old fella. I wish I did not have to do this.' Then he swiftly used his knife to kill the dog, but not before Spy bit him. Fighting tears, the doctor did the same to Moody, a lop-eared black and tan dog, and Watch, the youngest and fastest of his team. The other dogs watched from the other side of the ice pan. As quickly as he could with freezing fingers, he cut the fur coats off the dead dogs, piled up the bodies and made a shelter against the wind. Then he cut off the leg bones from two of the bodies and formed a flag pole, tying his outer shirt to it. Maybe someone would see it. Then calling the rest of the dogs to him, he huddled with them behind the shelter trying to stay warm.

As Dr. Grenfell sat, feeling drowsy with the cold, he thought about dying. He was surprised to find he was not afraid. He knew God was with him. Suddenly a verse of a hymn he had learned in school came into his mind: My God, my Father, while I stray

Far from my home on life's rough way,

Oh, help me from my heart to say,

Thy will be done.

He would leave the rescuing up to God, knowing that God knows best.

***

What Wilfred did not know was that someone did see him floating out to sea. Four fishermen were cutting up some seals late in the day and happened to look out and see something unusual on the ice. Not sure what it was, they returned to the village to ask the only person who owned a telescope to have a look. He thought he saw some shapes on the ice moving out to sea, but was not sure.

Later, when some men from the Mission hospital in St. Anthony came by inquiring if Dr. Grenfell had come through the village, the man told them what he saw. Immediately the fishermen began to organise a rescue party. They could not go out in the dark because it was too dangerous. They had to be able to see the pieces of ice to steer around them, or the ice would crush their boat.

So the next morning the boat left the shore with several men rowing and two men at the front. They knew how important it was to get to Wilfred. It was a highly dangerous situation that he was in. 'If we don't get to him soon he's as good as dead,' one man declared. These words urged the rescuers on as they gave every last bit of energy they had. They leaned out of the boat and, with poles, pushed the ice away from the prow. They made slow progress, and the pan with the doctor and his dogs seemed to be drifting further away.

Wilfred was so cold that he could not see very well the next morning, and was not sure if the black shape moving through the water was a boat or not. As the rescuers drew near, they shouted to the doctor to stay still. Wilfred needed no reminder. He could not move much at all. The dogs whimpered when they saw the men, but stayed where they were around Wilfred. Carefully several of the fishermen climbed on to the ice, one doing his best to hang on to the boat's rope to keep it alongside. The others in the boat watched to make sure the other pieces of ice did not knock against their craft. The first man gave Wilfred a drink of hot tea from a warmed bottle.

'Dr. Grenfell, sir. Are you okay? Let us help you to the boat.'

Wilfred did not even have the strength to reply, and made no attempt to get up on his feet. So the strong fishermen lifted him up and carried him to the boat. Then they went back for the dogs, who allowed themselves to be lifted in one by one. No-one made any comment about the grisly shelter of dog pelts that was left on the ice pan. Slowly the rescue boat made its way back to the shore.

Wilfred was taken to the hospital in St.

Anthony by dog sledge, and for a time everyone was worried whether he would recover. However, his frozen hands and feet did heal, and after three months he was able to resume his work.

Wilfred was delighted to hear the good news about his young patient. 'A boat got through?' he exclaimed, somewhat amazed.

'Yes, just a few days after they found you on the ice pan,' a colleague smiled. 'The ice had broken up enough by then to allow it through to St. Anthony. The boy is now being treated in the ward just down the corridor from here!'

Wilfred smiled and laughed a little. It was a strange ending to a rather sorry story. He was glad that the boy was better - but he would always be sorry about his dogs, Moody, Watch and Spy.

When Wilfred returned home, he wanted to let people know about what had happened to him on the ice pan. He missed his dogs terribly and still wished he had not had to kill them. Then he had an idea. He had a bronze plaque made and hung in his front hall where every visitor could see it when they came in. It read: To the memory of Three Noble Dogs - Moody, Watch, and Spy whose lives were given for mine on the ice. April 21st, 1908.

As Wilfred was recovering, he thought about how he had ended up as a missionary doctor so far from his home in England.

'As a boy I dreamed about being an explorer - but I never thought that I'd end up as a doctor in Labrador and Newfoundland. All I ever wanted was a life full of adventure. Now I have that and more!'

Wilfred certainly had never thought that serving God could be interesting at all. But God knew all along just the right job for Wilfred, and guided him to a more exciting life than he could ever imagine.

GROWING UP

'Race you to the shore!' Wilfred called out to his older brother. They were both swimming in the sea just off the west coast of England. Their small village of Parkgate sat at the head of the River Dee and the Welsh mountains could be seen in the distance. Algernon took on the challenge without a word, swiftly cutting his way through the water. Wilfred followed, working hard to keep up. With much concentration he almost caught up with his brother but Algernon just edged ahead of Wilfred as the two boys raced out of the water on to the huge sandy beach, laughing as they went.

Algie had officially won, but Wilfred wrestled him to the ground and they called it a draw.

They lay on the sand, not bothered by the cool breeze, watching the sandpipers strutting about the beach.

'Know what we need?' Wilfred asked, as he pushed his thick mop of dark curly hair out of his eyes.

'Our guns to shoot those birds,' Algie replied, as the gulls screamed overhead.

'No. A boat. Every fisherman's boy has a boat at our age. I'm ten years old after all. Just think where we could go with a boat.'

'We are not fishermen's boys. Father is a headmaster and a minister, and not much interested in the sea. Besides, where would we get a boat?'

Wilfred thought in silence for a moment. 'We could build one,' he said at last.

His brother liked the idea. It was just the project they needed for the summer. Their parents were away on holiday and although the school matron was in charge of the boys, she rarely saw them during the day. The boys were always busy exploring and swimming and now they were going to build a boat!

Home for Wilfred and his brothers was Mostyn House, a school where his father was headmaster. Algernon was two years older than Wilfred and they had a younger brother called Cecil. Cecil did not play with his brothers because of an accident when he was very young. A nurse cared for him. Their fourth brother had died of meningitis when he was seven. So Algie and Wilfred were boyhood companions, getting into all kinds of scrapes together. They had unusual freedom for children their age. Their parents travelled to Switzerland every summer, leaving their two oldest sons to roam the countryside and get to know the fisherman along the coast. The boys' escapades were the talk of the town.

But Algie and Wilfred were not sure whether Matron would allow them to build the boat, so rather than ask her, they decided to build it in secret in the night nursery. Finding the necessary wood from their fishermen friends, they set about making a coffin-shaped flat bottom canoe. They would disappear for hours, banging nails and waterproofing their craft. Once they were finished they decided to name it *Reptile*. There was only one problem. It was too big to go out the door.

'Now what do we do?' Algie asked. 'We can't leave it here.'

Wilfred looked at the window and grinned. 'That is bigger than the door. Why not take out the frame and glass and launch it through there?'

So they waited until night-time and set to work dismantling the frame and removing the glass, carefully laying out the pieces to be replaced later. Then the boys lifted the boat up over the frame and lowered it down outside. With the window back in place, the boys hauled the boat down to the water's edge and gave it a proper launching into the sea. Such freedom they had that summer, sailing along the coast by the mouth of the River Dee. The boat capsized once, but remained seaworthy for several years. They took the shotguns their father had given them and hunted the many kinds of birds that lived along the shore like pink-footed geese, oystercatchers, curlews and golden plovers.

Growing up by the sea had a great influence on Wilfred. He used to love to dive into the waters and let the current carry him to the banks at the mouth of the river. He knew no fear when it came to the ocean. Wilfred also liked to camp out at night by the shore. The smell of salt water and the cry of the birds gave Wilfred a feeling of contentment. He would go on long expeditions up the coastline when the tide was out, exploring all the channels and then swimming part of the way home.

Wilfred loved the sea. However, he did not like school. Or more correctly, Wilfred did not like to study. If there were games to play, he was the first in line. A natural athlete, he loved to play any team sport. It was not that Wilfred was a stupid boy. In fact, many things interested him. During the times he was exploring he collected insects and birds. He found the world around him fascinating. But sitting still and trying to memorise facts and figures was not Wilfred's idea of fun. Life was meant to be lived with action.

Mr. Grenfell, Wilfred's father, despaired of his son. 'You have learned very little here,' he scolded one day. His father looked very stern peering through his glasses, his black curly beard shaking with every word. 'Algernon is a much better student than you.' Wilfred knew this was true. For all his pranks, Algie was a good student and was forgiven much as a result. 'You are thirteen now and it is time for you to go to boarding school. You will join your brother at Marlborough next term.'

Being sent away to Marlborough School in Wiltshire was hard for Wilfred. He was homesick and found the work difficult. Sulking in his dorm Wilf sighed to himself one evening. 'Algie's too busy with his studies to spend time with me,' Wilfred grumbled. 'I'm just his little brother - he prefers being with his school friends. He can't be bothered with me. On top of all that school is so dull - deadly dull in fact!' Wilfred grumbled to himself. But just then his face broke into a smile. 'At least the headmaster has made games compulsory! That was a good idea whoever thought that

one up. I'm good at games - excellent in fact!
I think team sports are my favourite though,
but I enjoy the new swimming pool. It's not a
patch on the sea, however. I wish I hadn't
had to leave the ocean behind me.' Wilfred
sighed once again and tried to get his head
round his Latin and history homework.

Wilfred was definitely a boy who preferred
action rather than study. Given a choice he
would go for football, rugby, cricket — even
running on the spot. Anything was better than
another hour in the library! And then one
morning as Wilfred looked in the mirror while
trying to tidy up his shock of unruly hair he
noticed something which quite pleased him.
'Hmm!' he thought to himself. 'I'm getting taller!
I'm sure of it... and broader.' He clenched the
muscles in one arm and pinched the skin with
the other. 'I'm definitely filling out,' he
exclaimed. Wilfred was growing into a young
man. 'All the better for beating the rivals at
sports,' he chuckled to himself.

But when Wilfred was sixteen he took ill
with a severe cough and sore chest, and could

not stay at the school for a term. 'Send that young man to a warmer climate,' was the doctor's orders. So Wilfred's parents sent him to his aunt in the south of France. His aunt was delighted to see him and she made sure he obeyed the doctor's orders to live out of doors as much as possible. Wilfred could not have asked for a better prescription. Two young girls, daughters of a family friend, roamed the countryside with him catching moths and butterflies and frogs. They mounted the butterflies in frames with labels, and kept the frogs in miniature ponds with netting. He was fascinated with how God had created each of the small insects and animals that he caught.

However, returning to school brought Wilfred little joy. His studies seemed even more difficult and it appeared that he would not be ready for university. So his father hired a tutor to try to prepare him for Oxford, where his brother was now studying. But what would Wilfred do with his life? 'The army sounds interesting and certainly exciting,' Wilfred mused. 'Becoming a minister might please father but I can't just become a minister or a missionary in the same way that I would become an engineer or a lawyer. You have to have a calling for a job like that.' Wilfred was very confused about what he should do until one day his father sent him to talk to the local doctor.

'Come in, come in, my boy,' Dr. Russell said. He was a kind and patient man. 'Your father tells me you have finished your studies at Marlborough school. So what do you plan to do now?'

'Well sir, I'm not sure. My father does not want me to go into the army, and I don't want to be a teacher like him. My brother is doing that.' Wilfred shrugged his shoulders. 'I'm not sure what to do.'

'Have you ever considered medicine? Why not come into my surgery and see some of the things I have there.'

Wilfred followed Dr. Russell through a door and into a very interesting room. For the first while Wilfred just wandered around, looking at the surgical instruments laid out on a table. They gleamed and some of them looked very sharp. Wilfred was about to ask what each was used for when he looked up at a shelf and forgot all about the instruments. There in a large jar was a strange object floating in some liquid. He looked round to see Dr. Russell smiling.

'Thought you might be interested in that,' he said, and reached up to lift the heavy jar down. 'Want a closer look?'

Wilfred took the jar carefully, turning it around to get a good look at the contents. 'What is it?'

'A brain. A human brain. Quite amazing, isn't it? Here let me show you what all the parts do. Our brains are like a ship's navigator for our bodies, giving out instructions and making sure all the parts of the body do their assigned job.'

For the next while, Dr. Russell talked about how the body works and Wilfred listened with fascination. It had never occurred to him that the human body was like a complex machine, so carefully put together by God. The more Dr. Russell talked, the more Wilfred asked and listened with pleasure. Here was a whole new area of study that he actually wanted to know about.

At the end of the afternoon, Dr. Russell observed, 'I think you have found your calling, my boy. The world can always use more doctors.'

So in February 1883, when Wilfred was eighteen, he entered the London Hospital Medical College.

When Wilfred went to London, his parents did too. After twenty years as headmaster, Wilfred's father decided to hire someone to run the school and he became a chaplain at the hospital. Unfortunately his health was not good. After only a year in the job he had to give it up. Wilfred tried to help his father feel better by taking him on a holiday to Norway in 1885, but it made no difference. Mr. Grenfell had to be admitted to a mental hospital shortly afterwards. He died there two years later. Wilfred was very sad about his father, and he worried about lots of things including his mother.

'Now that father is gone Mother is our responsibility,' he reminded Algie. Wilfred sighed. It was a heavy burden and a concern, but one that was made lighter when Mrs. Grenfell decided to move in with her sister for company, and Wilfred returned to his medical studies.

HEARING GOD'S CALL

'Don't you sleep?' Dennis Halstead asked his room mate, Wilfred. Dennis could hear the birds singing, but it was still dark. 'It can't be morning yet!' he complained. But Wilfred did not answer. He was too busy doing his morning exercises. Only after 50 push-ups did he stand up and look at Dennis, who was still wrapped up in his blankets.

'Lazy!' Wilfred declared with a grin. 'Up you get and wake up those muscles.' Wilfred tried to pull off Dennis's covers, but Dennis threw a pillow at him. Wilfred caught it and threw it back. 'Besides, you should be studying.'

Dennis sighed heavily. He really liked Wilfred and was happy to share lodgings with him while they both studied medicine at the

London Hospital Medical College. They also liked to do the same things. They both joined the rowing team, the rugby team and the cricket team. But there was one thing that Dennis did not like. Wilfred only needed six hours sleep a night and thought Dennis was lazy because he needed more.

Wilfred, full of energy, found sitting in a classroom to hear a lecture very difficult. He tried to study early in the morning as it was his best time of day. But he still struggled with the lectures.

'I can't give you a pass mark, Mr. Grenfell,' his Professor said. 'You only came to two lectures this term. You will have to study very hard for the exam and then you might pass.'

Wilfred could not argue. He knew he should do better but it was hard work to stay awake in most of the lectures. 'Some are very complicated and others are just far too boring.' Wilfred grimaced. He would much rather be in the hospital wards helping the patients. However, there was one doctor whose lectures Wilfred never missed. Professor

Treves was a brilliant surgeon and teacher. Always well dressed and gentlemanly, he lectured with enthusiasm on anatomy and surgery. He believed strongly in the new ideas of the time that helped to save many lives.

'Gentlemen, you can never be too clean when you are operating on a patient. Germs are everywhere. When you come into my theatre, you must scrub until your hands are glowing pink and touch nothing that will touch the patient. Otherwise I will have you thrown out.' Treves was very particular on hygiene, which was new for most doctors of that time.

He took a liking to Wilfred. They both were interested in sport and sailing as well as medicine. When Wilfred finished his medical training, Dr. Treves helped him to find his calling. Dr. Treves became Wilfred's hero.

Meanwhile, Wilfred learned by doing. He became a dresser, which meant he learned to care for wounds, fix broken bones, diagnose diseases and work out what to do to cure them. He learned how to do surgery by standing in the operating theatre and handing Dr. Treves the instruments he needed. He was on call to help patients who had serious injuries and needed help quickly. This was the kind of work that Wilfred enjoyed and he gained a great deal of valuable experience in the hospital wards.

Wilfred worked hard and eventually passed his exams in 1886. He went to Oxford for further study, but because he did not really like studying that much he spent a miserable first term there. He needed a different direction for his life. But Wilfred's new direction in life began before the exams and the further study he would undertake. He just didn't know it at the time. .

***

The year was 1885 and Wilfred had been visiting a patient in the poor district of Shadwell in London. As he was returning to the hospital, he passed a large tent and heard the sound of hymn singing. Curious, Wilfred went in. He had heard about the famous American evangelist D. L. Moody and he wanted to hear what he had to say. This was very different from the Church of England services he normally attended. Wilfred enjoyed the music that night, but became impatient with someone who started to pray and forgot to stop. The man went on so long that Wilfred thought he would just sneak out and go home. Suddenly, Mr. Moody, a big man with a curly black beard and a strong American accent, stood up and announced a hymn. He encouraged the congregation to join in. Then Wilfred sat down again and listened while Mr. Moody preached about serving God with our talents. Wilfred felt his heart starting to beat hard with excitement. He had grown up going to church regularly, but he had never thought about how he, Wilfred, should be serving God. Jesus Christ had died for him, giving his life so that Wilfred could be saved from sin. Now Wilfred should give his life to serve God. Wilfred left the tent that night full of hope and determination.

Later in the week he found time to go to more tent meetings. This time the famous cricket players J. E. and C. T. Studd were speaking. Again Wilfred heard God speaking to him through these men. They were athletes and spoke about using their gifts to serve God. Wilfred was amazed to hear that God wanted 'muscular Christians', people who worked hard at everything they did to bring glory to God. At the end of the service people were asked to stand if they were ready to follow Christ. Wilfred had never stood up in church like this before and he felt embarrassed. Then he saw a young sailor stand up and knew the ribbing that sailor would have to take from his mates. With a surge of courage he stood up too, declaring with that action that he was ready to follow Jesus Christ wherever he wanted Wilfred to go.

Wilfred was so excited he had to tell someone. His mother was the first person he thought of. She hugged and kissed him when he told her and then gave him some advice.

'Don't wait until you finish medical school. Be busy for God right now. Ask the minister what you can do in the church.'

Wilfred visited his minister the next day. The man could not have been more glad to hear of Wilfred's conversion or his willingness to do something to serve God.

'I have just the job for you,' the minister exclaimed. 'We need someone to teach a boys' Sunday school class. I think you could do that very well. It's a job that needs an enthusiastic, robust, young man!'

Wilfred was not so sure. He had never taught Sunday school before. If that is what God wants me to do, I'll try, he thought.

The next Sunday afternoon Wilfred met 'his boys'. They were a rough lot, most had no schooling and worked as apprentices in various shops and trades. They were not used to sitting still for a Bible lesson and several teachers had already given up on them. Wilfred knew this would be a challenge.

One Sunday, several weeks later, the boys were not listening to him teach the lesson. Wilfred knew he needed to do something.

'How many of you have done any boxing?' Wilfred suddenly asked.

The boys stopped their carrying on and stared at Wilfred.

'Why would we know about boxing?' one boy eventually asked.

Wilfred smiled. 'I'm going to teach you,' he announced. 'Meet at my house next Saturday evening. Come ready to learn how not to get knocked down.' With that statement, he dismissed the class.

Full of curiosity, all the boys turned up on Saturday. They discovered that Wilfred had turned his dining room into a boxing ring. He had several sets of gloves for the boys to share.

'Who is first?' Wilfred challenged.

Full of confidence, one of the biggest boys stepped up and stripped off his jacket. He strutted around the ring while he pulled on the gloves. All the boys began to cheer him on. But he soon discovered he had a lot to learn. Although a little shorter than the young man, Wilfred was quick and strong. He moved about the ring delivering unexpected blows. The boy began striking out but never hit his teacher. Wilfred let him try for a few minutes and then stunned him with a blow to the shoulder that sent him to the floor.

'Not as easy as it looks,' Wilfred said to them all. 'But I plan to teach every one of you to defeat me. You need to train your bodies and keep yourselves fit. And then you need to train your souls to serve God. We will do both every Saturday evening.'

It worked. The boys enthusiastically learned the boxing techniques and worked off excess energy. And then they also listened as Wilfred taught them from the Bible. By the end of that year the boys' class had grown so large that Wilfred did not have room for them all. And that was not the only problem.

The minister came to see Wilfred to tell him to stop the meetings. 'Your job is to teach the Bible to these boys, not boxing. The church cannot allow this to go on.'

Wilfred argued with the man, but to no avail. So Wilfred resigned from the Sunday school and kept up his work with the boys. He felt this was what God wanted him to do. They moved to a bigger place and carried on with their sports and Bible lessons.

'These boys need to see the sea,' Wilfred said to his brother, Algie, a year after the club had started. 'Most of them have never been outside London. Instead of just taking our usual summer holiday why not set up a seaside camp for these boys?'

Algie agreed. For the next few summers, with the help of some friends, the brothers organised summer camps. The boys had to save their money through the year to help pay for it, although Wilfred often paid for those who were too poor to save. They had a wonderful two weeks learning how to swim and navigate small boats on the sea. Wilfred or his brother led daily devotions. Dr. Treves allowed them to use his property in Dorset and he even came to teach the boys water polo. Wilfred enjoyed the camps as much as the boys did. He was back at the sea he loved and teaching others about God. What better combination could there be?

DOWN TO THE SEA

'Hello, is anyone there?' Wilfred called out from the wharf[1]. The tide was out and all that he could see of the *Thomas Gray* was its topmasts. The rest of the smack was hidden by the quay. The cold wind threw light mists of rain at Wilfred as the evening sky darkened.

'Hello,' a cheerful voice responded. 'Welcome aboard, Dr. Grenfell.'

Smiling, Wilfred lowered his bags down to some waiting hands. A sturdy wooden structure, called a stay, looked just the thing for him to grab hold of and slide down onto the deck of the ship.

'Wait,' the cheerful voice called out again. 'That's just been greased and tarred.'

But it was too late. Wilfred was already

[1]A waterfront platform for docking and loading ships.

sliding down in fits and starts. His clothing was covered in grease by the time he found the deck. But even though he was filthy, the little smack[2] was spotless and her crew was friendly.

It was January 1888 and Wilfred was about to begin his first voyage as doctor for the Royal National Mission to Deep Sea Fishermen. Dr. Treves, his professor in medical school, was a Christian and medical advisor to the Mission. He had come to Wilfred a few months earlier with an exciting idea.

'I know this will suit you perfectly,' Dr. Treves had said. 'Our Mission needs a doctor who loves the ocean. He would sail on a hospital ship to the North Sea and treat any fishermen who become ill or have an accident. But we also want someone who is a Christian, who can tell them about God and his love for them.'

Wilfred could hardly believe what he was hearing. This was the perfect job for him. He had finished his studies and was tired of living in London. City life was not for him. He

44   [2] Another word for a sailing vessel

wanted to go back to the sea. And now Dr. Treves was asking him to join a sailing ship and be a doctor at the same time. Wilfred knew this was from God

'I can get my things together tonight and be ready tomorrow morning,' he declared.

Dr. Treves laughed. 'I thought you would say that. The ship is at Yarmouth. They are still fitting her with all the supplies you will need. Take the train down and have a look at her. You will be leaving just after the New Year.'

'A winter voyage?'

'The worst time of year, I am afraid. This will not be easy, but then you have never been afraid of hard work.'

Wilfred could hardly wait.

And it was hard work. Wilfred thought he was a good sailor, but soon changed his mind. He had never been in such rough storms. Gales blew day after day. He experienced seasickness for the first time. The rains quickly turned to snow, and ice formed on every surface of the smack when the temperatures began to fall. Wilfred tried to use the kerosene heater in his cabin, but it smelled so bad it made him feel worse. None of the crew were complaining, so Wilfred would not either. Instead he began to do some strange things, or at least the crew thought so.

Every morning he would get a bucket of sea water and take a cold shower with it. Then once he was dried and dressed he ran up and down on the deck, filling his lungs with lots of fresh air. It helped to take away the queasy feeling in his stomach.

'That doctor is daft!' one sailor observed.

'He'll die of cold or fall overboard long before we ever reach the fishing fleet,' another commented, shaking his head. 'What sort of doctor does such crazy things?'

Soon Wilfred began to get his sea legs; and just in time, for they finally spotted the fleet on the horizon. The fleet was made up of a huge number of fishing trawlers[3], all bouncing up and down on the rough sea. They sailed together with their nets dragging through the waters, pulling in catch after catch

46

[3] Another name for a fishing boat

of fish. Once the holds were full, the trawlers would send their catch over to the clippers[4] that waited close by. Then the clippers rushed the fish to London to sell in the markets. This way the fleet could keep fishing. It was hard work and the fishermen spent many months at sea.

'Hoist the blue banner,' the skipper[5] on the *Thomas Gray* called out. 'Let them know we are open for business.' One of the crew scampered to obey. 'And keep well away from those coper ships. I want the men only to come to us.'

The ship's navigator did as he was told. One of the reasons the Mission had sent the *Thomas Gray* was to stop the fishermen from going to the coper ships, which sold alcohol at a cheap price. Drinking was a very serious problem among the fishermen and it caused many accidents and deaths each year. The Mission wanted to provide a better place for them, where they could get medical help and warm clothing, and hear the gospel too.

Wilfred had never been so busy. The

[4] A fast commercial sailing ship.   [5] Captain of the ship   47

fishermen boarded the Mission ship with many problems. Some had broken bones from being tossed about on the decks, some had festering sores from the chafing of the oilskin coats. There were lots of cuts from gutting the fish and all sorts of diseases caused by bad food, bad hygiene and living in wet clothing all the time. But Wilfred was surprised that few of them complained. They liked living on the sea.

'Bring those barrels in here,' Wilfred directed the crew. The sailors had no idea why the doctor wanted heavy barrels in his surgery but they did as they were told. 'Place them side by side with a small space in between. Good. That should do the trick. Now my good man,' Wilfred turned to a fisherman nursing his swollen jaw, 'just step between those barrels and we will push them together to hold you into place.'

What was the doctor doing now? Wilfred smiled at their bewildered faces, opened up his medical bag and took out his instruments for extracting teeth.

'Those barrels will keep you still while I pull out that nasty tooth.'

And he was right. Even though the ship rocked back and forth with the swell of the sea, the fisherman stayed still wedged in between the barrels. Swiftly, Wilfred reached into the man's mouth and gave a mighty yank. Out came the tooth before the fisherman could even yell.

'Now we will stop the bleeding and you will be as right as rain.'

Wilfred developed his own procedures for sewing up bad cuts and other minor surgery. It may not have been the way he was taught in the Hospital, but it solved the problem on board ship. You had to change things, be flexible and be a problem solver when you were working in such a hostile environment.

As well as treating their bodies, Wilfred also treated their souls. He would tell stories about Jesus, especially the ones about the disciples who were fishermen too. The men sat and drank mugs of hot tea while Wilfred spoke. They took Christian books and magazines back with them to their trawlers to read and share with their shipmates.

When the fleet was fishing, the Mission ship would fish too. They pushed out their nets and watched as the net sank beneath the water. When the Admiral of the fleet hoisted the signal flag, all the ships began to haul in their catches. Wilfred rolled up his sleeves and joined in. He was strong enough to help pull in the heavy nets that were alive with cod. As the net swung in over the deck, showers of water and fish rained down. Some hands checked the nets for damage and repaired them while others were busy gutting the fish and stowing them in barrels.

Wilfred thought this was as much fun as hunting, and the crew was impressed that a doctor would help them. They began to change their minds about Wilfred. By the end of the voyage they treated him just like one of the crew.

When Wilfred returned from his voyage, he reported to the National Mission to Deep Sea Fishermen about all the medical cases he had treated and how he had shared the gospel with the men. After several more voyages Wilfred went to the Mission Council with more than just a report.

'There is still so much more that needs to be done,' he added. 'One Mission ship is not enough for the whole fleet. We must have a fleet of our own so that all the fishermen can be treated. And we need to keep them away from the evil influences of the coper ships and the drink they sell. Now, I have all sorts of ideas. Besides getting more smacks and more doctors, we need to have places on land for the fishermen to visit instead of the taverns[6]. When they go there they only waste their pay on drink. If we had a hall where they could get good food and good companionship, think of how many men and their families would be kept from alcohol. We could have Christian literature for them to read and regular speakers.'

The Mission committee were smiling while Wilfred went on for some time with his list of ideas. By the time he was finished, the Council

[6] An old fashioned pub where alcohol was sold.

offered him the job of Superintendent and told him to go ahead with his plans. Wilfred, now twenty-four years old, got to work right away.

First of all he moved to Gorleston, which became his headquarters. The townspeople did not know what to make of him.

'He doesn't even sleep in a bed,' his landlady reported to her neighbours. 'He sleeps on the floor in a sleeping bag. And he goes out every morning to swim in the sea. I do worry about his safety. He takes that canvas canoe out in all kinds of weather. It's a wonder he doesn't get lost in the fog.'

They had to admit he was friendly though, and he talked about the Mission at every opportunity. He was never still. When he was not working at headquarters, he was touring towns and villages speaking in churches and raising money for the work.

'Dr. Grenfell, that was a wonderful talk you gave tonight,' one of the Mission workers said. 'You have a real gift for making us feel we are right there on the Mission ship with you. Have you ever thought of writing down your stories so that even more people can hear them? That way so many more people would hear of this work we are doing for God.'

Wilfred had not thought about writing before, but once he started it came as easily as telling his yarns on board ship. He supplied the Mission magazine with many exciting stories from the North Sea.

Wilfred also began to think about others who might need help. It came to his attention that the herring fishermen off the Irish coast needed medical ships. So he mounted an expedition to investigate. He sailed along the coast and walked along it as well, making notes on the fishing methods and keeping records for the Marine Biological Society. He surprised the local people by sleeping wherever he found himself at night, in barns and stables far more than in houses. He made many friends on his travels and came back to Gorleston with more plans for the Mission Council.

In Gorleston the new fishermen's hall opened with a coffee bar, reading room, library, classroom and recreation room. Wilfred wanted to have classes for the fishermen and their families to teach first aid, navigation, reading and writing. He started a brass band, a boys' club and summer camp. He wanted the children of the fishermen to have good things to do to keep them out of trouble.

'What will that doctor think of next?' people kept asking. 'He is so kind. There just doesn't seem to be enough he can do.'

And they were right. Wilfred did need more to do. So in 1891, when he heard about yet more fishermen that needed his help, he was ready to sail on to a new adventure.

ACROSS THE ATLANTIC

'It looks like the whole town is on fire!' one of the sailors called out. Wilfred and the others aboard the *Albert* rushed to the deck to see. Even though they were still a day from the St. John's harbour in Newfoundland, they could see the flames and smoke. What disaster were they sailing into?

It was 1892, and Wilfred was on his way to investigate the fisheries off the coast of Canada. It was a long journey across the Atlantic Ocean, but since Newfoundland was still a colony of Great Britain the Mission wanted to help the fishermen there too. The fisheries had been running in Newfoundland since the eighteenth century, with the fishermen sailing across the ocean in the spring and returning to England in the autumn. However, over the years many decided to stay and live there all year round. They married local women and began to raise their families along the coast of Labrador. It was these people, called Liveryer, that Wilfred wanted to meet.

As the *Albert* lay off the harbour, the crew could see flames surrounding the town and columns of smoke that rose into the sky. The evening sky was darkening and it was too dangerous to navigate between the narrow cliff-walled entrance, so the ship waited until morning to be towed in. But they had plenty to see. A huge iceberg floated by, then turned over and broke into pieces with a loud boom, throwing large waves toward the *Albert*. The crew watched as the chunks of ice dispersed in the ocean currents. Then a whale leapt out of the water and sent more waves their way. It was a magnificent welcome. Much nicer scenery than the poor town of St. John's.

As they were towed into the harbour, Wilfred saw a scene of destruction. All the wooden buildings had been burnt to the ground. Only stone chimneys stood upright marking the spots where houses had been. Most of the stone buildings had been gutted. The fire in the town itself was out, but the surrounding tree-covered hills were still ablaze. Eleven thousand people were homeless. Fortunately there were no deaths.

Wilfred and his Mission crew got right to work. They had not come to help these people, but Wilfred could not ignore their needs.

'Unpack some of those clothing bales,' he ordered. The *Albert* was full of second hand clothing donated by churches in England. 'We will help as many people as we can. They have lost everything in this fire.'

Wilfred also set up a temporary medical clinic on board to help out the local doctors who were busy tending to all the injuries and burns that the people had suffered.

'Thank you so much for all your help, Dr. Grenfell. God must have sent you. You arrived just at the right time,' said Sir William

Whiteway, the Premier of Newfoundland. 'But I know you want to be on your way to the coast of Labrador. I have found a pilot for you. The waters are not well charted and the currents are very tricky, but Captain Fitzgerald knows the coast well and will be a good guide for you.'

'Thank you,' Wilfred replied. 'I am anxious to see Labrador and meet its people.' So a month after arriving in St. John's, the *Albert* sailed north.

At first they saw very little because the ship was shrouded in fog, a common problem on the coast. When it cleared, Wilfred gazed on a place very different from the shore at home. The mainland was made of sheer rock cliffs, with scores of rocky treeless islands, some large, others small, covered in blue moss. The waves of the ocean crashed against them with a steady rhythm, and beyond them, huge icebergs drifted lazily in the currents.

'What a desolate place,' complained one of the crew.

'No,' said Wilfred, the strong breezes

blowing in his face. 'It's magnificent. There is nothing soft or pretty here, but it is beautiful all the same. Look at the colours of all the different rocks in those cliffs. And those whales over there! Have you ever seen such wonderful creatures?'

Navigating amongst all those islands with their treacherous currents was indeed a challenge. Wilfred was very glad of Captain Fitzgerald's ability. He took them from settlement to settlement, coming so close to rocks at times that the crew thought they were sure to hit them, but each time they came safely through.

Sitting back to take stock of recent events Wilfred marvelled at what had been accomplished. 'We've visited fifty settlements in two months. Transportation has meant that sometimes we've sailed right into the natural harbours but other times, when it has been too shallow for the *Albert,* we've had to resort to being ferried in by smaller vessels. Everyone in the settlements has received us with such excitement. It makes all the hard work worthwhile just to see their joyful faces as we come on shore.'

One afternoon as Wilfred arrived at one of the settlements there was the usual crowd of eager patients waiting for treatment. He soon dealt with some of the minor injuries and then he worked on the more serious cases.

'We've never had a doctor here, nor a minister neither,' one man explained as he ushered Wilfred through the door of his cabin 'Can you really help my wife? She has been ever so poorly this year.'

Wilfred looked down at the woman lying in the wooden bunk built into the side of the cabin. Her leg was covered in sores that oozed.

'I'll have those sores cleaned and dressed in a trice,' he smiled encouragingly, but inwardly he sighed. What she really needed was proper nursing for several months to make sure the leg healed. Looking around the cabin, Wilfred knew they could not afford a nurse or a hospital even if one were close by. The only furniture other than the built-in beds was a table and some wooden crates. The family's few possessions hung on hooks by the door.

'We have some clothing on board ship for the children,' he said as he worked. The entire family had gathered round to watch Wilfred work. From the youngest to the oldest the children were dressed in tattered trousers and shirts.

'Why not bring them to the ship later on and get some new boots for yourself while you're at it,' he added, noticing the sorry state of the man's footwear. 'We're holding a prayer meeting this evening and you are all welcome to come.'

The ship was designed to open up its folding doors in the hold and there was room for a hundred people to gather. The prayer meeting began with hymn singing accompanied by an organ. The crew, all members of the Mission, led the people with their strong voices. Wilfred, dressed in a tweed hunting suit, prayed and preached. Everyone listened with careful attention while Wilfred told them about Jesus and his love for sinners.

The service finished with several of the Mission crew praying and reading from the Bible.

'That was lovely, Doctor,' a woman came up to Wilfred afterwards. 'How much you must love Jesus to come all this way to us. Please may I have a Bible?'

Wilfred gladly handed out Bibles and Christian books and magazines to whoever wanted them. By the end of the voyage they had given away all of the clothing and Christian literature. Wilfred had treated over seven hundred people and held many prayer services both on land and aboard ship. When he arrived back in England in November he had many stories to tell.

'You should see how these people live,' he told the Mission Council meeting. 'Some of the settlements are perched on bare rock so they can be close to the sea for their work. And work they do, even when they are ill. They live in huts and have very little food. They do not eat much of the fish they catch because they owe the merchants for the fishing boats and equipment they bought on credit. They have to sell the fish to pay their debts. I can't tell you how grateful these people were to see us and we had so little to offer. They need doctors and nurses and hospitals. They need ministers and churches. They need so much it is hard to know where to begin. This I do know. I am going back next summer with two doctors and two nurses and as many supplies as we can carry. Their voices are calling out to us to help them. How can we enjoy our plenty here when they have so little?'

Wilfred was out of breath by the time he sat down. He got so worked up about the needs of Labrador he almost forgot to stop talking. When he looked around at the Council members, only a few were nodding in agreement. Others looked distressed.

'Dr. Grenfell, we understand your concern for these people and we wish we could do more. However, our funds are limited. We have already used most of our money for the North Sea and the Irish fleets. We do not have enough to start a third mission on a long term basis. We have a letter from Newfoundland saying they will build two hospitals for the Mission, but we have to staff them and keep them running. Where will the money come from?'

Wilfred was not deterred. 'I will raise the money myself. I will tour England to tell the people about Labrador. I am sure the Lord will provide the money.'

'But what about your other responsibilities? You need someone to take over in Gorleston if you are going to be on a speaking tour.'

Wilfred did not argue. He was so excited about the needs of Labrador that he wanted to work for those people first. And besides, he was not really interested in sitting at a desk in Gorleston. He wanted to be involved in this new challenge. So it was arranged. If Wilfred could raise the money and find volunteers, he could plan a second voyage.

Wilfred worked very hard. He spoke every night at meetings throughout England, and the people were touched by the stories of poverty, illness and the isolated life of the fishermen. Over that winter load after load of medical supplies, clothing and books were donated. Money came pouring in for the hospitals and two more doctors volunteered their services along with two nurses. God answered all the needs, and someone donated enough money to build a new steam ship. Wilfred could hardly wait to start sailing it.

When Wilfred returned to St. John's in 1893, a tremendous welcome awaited him. News of his first voyage had been written up in the newspapers as an 'Angel Visit', and people in Canada had read about the Mission's work. The people of Newfoundland and Labrador were very grateful that 'The Doctor' had returned. The two promised hospitals had been built, one at Battle Harbour and the other further north at Indian Harbour. All that summer the Battle Harbour hospital was full and the medical staff worked very hard. People in this area of southern Labrador had never had access to a hospital before, and now instead of living with, or even dying from their illnesses, they could be treated.

Meanwhile, Wilfred and another doctor

sailed up the coast taking the same route that Wilfred had taken the year before. Once more the isolated communities were thrilled to see the Doctor, as they now called Wilfred. They brought out their sick, pleading with him to make them well so they could return to fishing. They gratefully accepted the clothing and books, and most came to hear the gospel preached.

By November, it was time for the team to return to England. But Wilfred had other plans. He set out to begin a speaking tour of Canada. He spoke at churches and societies in Nova Scotia, where the newspapers took up the cause and encouraged people to come out and hear Wilfred. In Montreal, some influential people had already heard about the Mission's work and were prepared to donate a ship, and more money so that Wilfred could travel as far as Vancouver to tell about his work. Wilfred was welcomed everywhere he went and people formed societies to raise money to send to the work in Labrador.

Wilfred was overwhelmed with the

generosity. He wrote to his mother and told her all about the tour and then he wrote the Mission and told them. Wilfred's mother was pleased and proud of the work her son was doing. She also liked the furs he sent her and had them made into a warm coat.

For the next three years Wilfred sailed back and forth across the Atlantic with more volunteer doctors and nurses. Both hospitals were full throughout the season, and a mission hall was constructed next to the Battle Harbour hospital. Each year when the ice blocked in the northern coastline, Wilfred took some time to travel and speak to as many churches and societies as would have him.

In the winter of 1895-96, instead of returning home as usual he began a tour in the United States. On his return there was a message from the Mission asking him to come to England. Wilfred was puzzled, but did as he was told.

'Dr. Grenfell, we appreciate all the work you have been doing, but you are still Superintendent of the Mission's work in the

North Sea. You must pay some attention to the work there. We want you to let Dr. Willway take over from you in Labrador so that you can get back to the work you are supposed to be doing.'

Wilfred was stunned. 'They're asking me to leave Labrador!' he gasped. 'I can't imagine leaving these people. I've grown to love them and respect them. But I have to accept the Mission Council's decision.'

Later that year Wilfred stood at the stern of a ship heading out of St. John's harbour. Dr. Willway was waving from the pier and Wilfred wiped a discreet tear from his eye. He had introduced the new overseer to the mission that had been his idea and vision. 'He knows what has to be done,' Wilfred thought to himself. 'And now I have to leave with a heart full of sadness.'

Wilfred gave one last wave of farewell to his good friends on the Labrador coast as the ship left the shelter of the harbour for the open sea.

THE LURE OF
LABRADOR

'Dr. Grenfell, we have had a letter from Dr. Willway. He wants to return to England because his wife is ill and needs treatment. He requested that you be sent in his place.'

Wilfred almost shouted for joy when the Mission Council told him the news. He had missed his beloved Labrador so much.

For the last two years Wilfred had spent his time with the Mission ships on the North Sea, overseeing the work in Gorleston, checking on the work on the Irish coast and even sailing to Iceland to see British sailors there. He raised funds to open more mission halls in Grimsby, Aberdeen, Fleetwood and Milford Haven so the fishermen could spend their time in better places than pubs.

At the same time, Wilfred also appealed for funds for a new hospital ship for Labrador. He had kept in touch with Dr. Willway and knew it was needed. So in 1899, when Dr. Willway wrote the Mission and announced he was coming back to England, it seemed only right that Wilfred should go in his place.

'I can take Dr. Grenfell's place in the North Sea while my wife gets the care she needs in England.' Dr. Willway suggested. 'And since he has already raised the funds for the *Strathcona*, the new hospital ship, he should be the one to sail her to Labrador.'

However, the new steamer was not ready on time and Wilfred had to content himself with arriving in Newfoundland on an ore-carrying[1] steamer instead. It wasn't till the following year that the new ship arrived in Labrador.

The entire town of Battle Harbour turned out to welcome Wilfred back. They gathered at the pier waving flags and shouting. It had been three years since he had left. Someone even fired off a gun salute. Wilfred almost cried

70 [1] Ore is a rock. Valuable metals can be extracted from it.

with joy as he walked through the crowd, shaking hands with the smiling fishermen and their families. The hospital had just been enlarged and freshly painted, and had new plumbing installed. Walking through the wards, Wilfred spoke with many of the patients.

'It is amazing to think that a large number of these men and women would be dead were it not for the hospital,' Wilfred thought to himself as he did the rounds. 'And then there are all the medical staff - doctors and nurses. They are a good team,' Wilfred realised. Out of the corner of his eye he spotted one of the doctors and called him over.

'How wonderful it is to see how well you have carried on the work here,' he said to Dr. Apsland. 'You and your wife have given up much to come and work here, and God will bless you for that. We must be sure that each one of these patients hears the gospel while we care for their bodies.'

Dr. Apsland smiled in agreement. It was good to have Wilfred Grenfell back in charge.

Wilfred spent that winter in St. Anthony at the very tip of Newfoundland, situated just below the Strait of Belle Isle and the Labrador coast. St. Anthony was a small village of seventeen families and the people there had suffered a terrible winter and much sickness the year before. So Wilfred stayed the winter with them to oversee the building of a hospital and organise some basic medical care.

***

'I need to learn how to use a dog sledge,' Wilfred announced one day. 'Walking even in snowshoes or on skis in this snow is too slow. I have watched those komatiks[2] race along with the dogs pulling and I want to do that too.'

Rueben Sims, a trapper and fisherman, sighed. He knew there was no arguing with the Doctor when he made up his mind about something. 'I'll teach you,' he agreed. 'But it is not an easy thing to control a team of eight dogs and a sixteen-foot komatik.'

Wilfred, smiling as always at a new challenge, said, 'Let's not waste time talking.

[2] Sledges with crossbars bound with animal skins.

I'm sure I will be an expert in no time.'

He wasn't, but he did not give up. First Wilfred met the team of dogs and learned how to hook them up to their traces.[3] The dogs were supposed to spread out in a fan shape and pull the sledge quickly over the ice and snow. It was up to the driver to shout directions to them and use his thirty foot lash to correct them. Many times Wilfred ended up in a snow bank, with the komatik overturned and the dogs tangled in a snarling mess. He even managed to wrap the sledge around a tree when half of the dogs ran one way around and the other half ran the other way. Wilfred leapt off just in time.

'It is a wonder that you are not in hospital,' Reuben muttered as he helped Wilfred to his feet. 'At this rate, I will have no komatik left.'

'Don't worry, my friend,' Wilfred assured him, stretching out his sore muscles. 'I almost have the knack of it now and I will buy the sledge from you. I plan to use it often to visit my patients during the winter months.'

And he did. He flew over the snow of

[3] The two side straps that connect a harness to the sledge.

Newfoundland to visit anyone who asked. The Northern part of Newfoundland and across the ice-covered Strait into Labrador were where he travelled to most. His journeys were sometimes as far as thirty miles. After he had seen to his patient one of the best parts of these visits was to sit around the fire with the fishermen and hear stories about their lives. They laughed together and sang the folksongs that had been passed down from their ancestors. And at the end of each evening, Wilfred always prayed with them and read a story from the Bible. He could never leave a place without speaking about Jesus Christ, who had sent him. He loved these people and they loved him ... he prayed that they would love Christ more.

One day, not long before Christmas Wilfred was visiting a family he knew, but something puzzled him.

'Why aren't you all outside in the fresh air?' Wilfred demanded. Ignoring their protests at the frigid weather, he herded the men and children outside. 'Come on,' he urged. 'The ice on the harbour is frozen solid. Let's organise a football game. I'll mark out the boundaries while you get the players organised.'

It worried Wilfred that so many of the people spent their winters inside their dreary homes with nothing to do until the spring thaw came and the fishing season began. They had no extra money to spend on entertainment. There was nothing for them to do so Wilfred turned the courthouse into a hall where people could gather to play games, read and visit with one another. He got the children to help him decorate the walls with pictures from old magazines and printed Bible verses. He organised the young men into groups and took them out for a day of hunting. The young men enjoyed themselves and it also helped to feed the village.

'Now we must do something special for Christmas day itself,' Wilfred announced. 'I need some strong young men to help me cut down an evergreen tree and set it up in the centre of the village. Then we can decorate it.'

The children, full of excitement, busied themselves making and hanging the decorations. The day itself was marked with the entire village gathering to play games on the ice and then a dinner and prize-giving in the courthouse.

Wilfred's sense of fun and adventure was infectious and soon the people were drawing together into a community. They spent that winter working together to chop trees for the new hospital so that all would be ready to build in the spring.

***

'The *Strathcona* has arrived,' the message read.

This was the news Wilfred had been waiting for. The new hospital ship was docked at Battle Harbour awaiting his return from his summer trip up the coast of Labrador.

'What a beauty she is,' Wilfred repeated over and over again as the crew took him on a tour. 'What an answer to prayer. We have a proper dispensary, x-ray equipment and even a bathroom!'

'Look at the electric lights, sir,' one of the crew said, pointing out the switch. 'And,' he added proudly, 'her hull is steel plated to withstand the pressure of ice, should we be caught in an ice floe.'[4]

Wilfred happily sailed the *Strathcona* up and down the coast of Labrador visiting his patients. Many times he was able to save limbs and lives, and the people were grateful. Sometimes he was too late: the disease had gone too far or the patient was too weak to have an operation. People often lived so close to starvation that they didn't have the strength to fight illness.

'Are all these children yours?' Wilfred asked a weary-looking mother.

'No,' she sighed. 'My neighbour lost her husband at sea last month, so she asked me to care for three of her children. She had very little food and no money. Then she died last week and so did her baby. I don't know what to do. I would dearly like to have them all here, Doctor, but my husband can barely find enough food for us. Could you take them?'

[4] A sheet of floating ice

Wilfred did not hesitate. 'Which ones are they?' he asked, and three sad, pale, young boys stepped forward. Wilfred reached out to them and wrapped all three in a big hug. 'God, your heavenly Father has sent me to take you to a new home. We will sail there on my ship. Will you come?'

The youngest did not look so sure, but his brothers smiled and nodded.

'What are you going to do with all these children?' a nurse asked Wilfred when he returned. He had collected several other orphans, two who were blind and a girl who had lost both her feet to frostbite. 'We'll care for them at the hospital until they're all well, of course, but then where will they live? Not with you, Doctor. You are away too much of the time. They need proper homes.'

Wilfred agreed and he already had a plan. 'When I go on my speaking tour at the end of the fishing season. I will tell the churches in Canada and the United States about this need. I am sure God will supply homes and money to build an orphanage.'

And he did. Several families asked to adopt the orphans and Wilfred accompanied the children to their new homes and saw them settled. Then he set about finding the right person to run his children's home once it was built.

'It really is a children's home, and not just an orphanage,' Wilfred explained to Eleanor Storr, a volunteer from New England. 'We will take in any child who is in need. Some families have fifteen or twenty children. The parents can't afford to feed them all. These children are welcome too. Every child should have clean clothes, a warm loving place to live and a chance to go to school. Would you be willing to run such a home?'

Miss Storr agreed, and in 1905 the first children's home was opened in St. Anthony. Next Wilfred planned to build schools, not just for these children, but up and down the coast, so that all the children could have some education. However, not everyone was pleased with that idea or others that Wilfred had and they began to make life difficult for him.

CHANGING THINGS

'We already have a school here, Dr. Grenfell. We don't need another.' The Anglican priest shook his finger at Wilfred.

'Yes, you do,' Wilfred replied, trying not to lose his temper. 'Your school is only for those in your church and meets only two mornings a week. All the children need a chance to get an education and they need more than just your church's religious classes.'

'You have no teachers and no buildings. And how will the people afford to send their children? Stick to being a doctor and leave other matters alone.'

But Wilfred would not leave the school idea alone. He had plans, if only he could get the help he needed.

The Newfoundland government was not interested in starting up new schools in the isolated communities. It would cost too much to build them and then pay teachers to live and teach there. Wilfred would have to look elsewhere.

Deeply concerned for the children, Wilfred began to include their stories in the fund-raising talks he gave. After he had told churches, colleges and universities of the need, help began to arrive.

First the money arrived to build a school in St. Anthony. A lady from Chicago sent enough money for the building and to pay two teachers. Later more money arrived from a lady in Texas to build a school in Cartwright, a small village close to Indian Harbour. Teachers arrived too, some of whom were willing to work without pay. Wilfred was so thankful for God's provision.

But the criticism from the church leaders and the government officials did not stop.

'You are not teaching the right things. These children won't be able to pass the Colony examinations. You have to teach all the subjects on our list.'

Wilfred agreed, with a few exceptions. 'Our teachers will teach most of the subjects, but not all. Latin and French are fine for city folk, but here the children need to learn to work with their hands as well as their heads. Most of them will stay here all their lives and they need to earn a living.'

Even when the schools became a success the criticism did not stop. But Wilfred didn't stop.

***

'The truck system is so wrong! These people are kept in debt by the merchants year after year and it only gets worse.' Wilfred was angry. He had arrived at a home where several of the children had already died from malnutrition and the rest of the family were very weak.

At the beginning of each fishing season the merchants in St. John's would advance supplies to the fishermen, and would wait to be paid at the end of the season. The fishermen hoped to get a good catch each year to pay off their debts to the merchants, but it did not always work that way.

'We have no food left,' the fisherman said sadly, 'and no money to buy anything. I settled with the merchant last week and he won't give me any more money for the winter. The fishing was poor this year and I couldn't pay for all the equipment he loaned me at the beginning of the season. My debt is now over $1000. I can never earn enough to pay him back and each year he adds on interest.'

'Then let's go hunting, Jim,' Wilfred suggested.

It was late autumn and there were still ducks flying south for the winter.

'I'll take my gun and we will get a few. They make a good meal.'

The fisherman shook his head. 'It will only be one meal. Then what do we do?'

The despair in the man's voice was almost more than Wilfred could bear. It was wrong to have people starving and in such debt that all they could do was give up. Wilfred had to think of a way to help them, and this meant meddling in the way people did business.

'The merchants aren't going to like this, Doctor. Are you sure we can't get into trouble?' The fishermen of Red Bay, on the north shore of the Strait, had met together to discuss forming a cooperative.

'This is just the venture you need,' Wilfred assured them. 'Rather than going to the merchants for food, clothing and equipment, put all your own money together, buy what you need and share it. And when you sell your fish at the end of the season, you all share in the profit. With that money you can buy food and supplies for the winter.'

It seemed like a good idea, but the fishermen were still afraid. They did not have much money to start the cooperative. So Wilfred lent them what they needed for the first year.

The Hudson's Bay Company was not pleased. The Company was made up of a group of merchants from England and Canada who had been given trading rights in Labrador and Newfoundland as far back as 1752. As far as The Company was concerned, all sales of equipment and food should come through them. They were not about to give up their profits without a fight and complained to the government of Newfoundland. They accused Wilfred of trying to make money for himself instead of trying to help the people of Labrador. So Wilfred coaxed one of the fishermen in the cooperative to handle all the money and organisation. He only took from the cooperative the money he lent them that first year. After that the fishermen were on their own to run their own store.

Once the cooperative store worked in Red Bay, then other communities asked to set up their own stores. By 1905, there were four stores established and several more being planned. Wilfred would only tell them how to do it, and then he left it to each village to make it work. Wilfred wanted to avoid the accusations from the merchants and he wanted the people to handle their own affairs and become independent. But the criticism and complaints did not stop. Wilfred even lost a number of friends who were merchants and had supported the Mission until now.

***

'What a beautiful mat you have made.'

Wilfred was admiring a brightly coloured mat in a patient's home. He had come to treat some children for rickets and noticed the work their mother was doing. She had unravelled old pieces of yarn, dyed them with solution made from moss and hooked them into an old piece of sacking. 'People in the cities would pay good money for such a mat.'

'Really?' The woman looked surprised. 'I just made it to make my home look nicer. We can't afford much. I just use left-over scraps.'

An idea started to bubble away in Wilfred's head.

'Would you make more of these if you had enough materials? Maybe your older children could help. I could take them to the city and sell them for you and bring you back the money. Or better still, I will buy them from you so you will have the money right away.'

'It would be no trouble at all. We have so little to do in the winter months. My neighbours all make them too. Could they sell theirs?'

Wilfred left the village with a stack of mats fastened to his sledge. He drew designs of dogs, icebergs and sledges for the women to copy on to more mats, which he promised to pick up the next time he came to visit.

In another village he discovered some women wanted to make gloves and moccasins if only they had some deerskin. So when Wilfred travelled north to Hamilton Inlet, he bought deerskins from the Indians who camped there every summer. As Wilfred travelled south again he gave out the skins and received promises of moccasins and gloves that he could take to the city to sell later.

'These people are gifted in making crafts,' Wilfred told a group of people in Boston, who had come out to hear about the Mission work. 'It's a good way for them to make the extra money they need to feed and clothe their families. But they need someone to teach them more crafts, like weaving or pottery.'

'I know just the person you need,' one of the women in the audience said.

The next day she took Wilfred to the town of Marblehead, not far from Boston, where some doctors had set up a small workshop for their patients who needed something to do while they recovered from their illnesses.

'This is Jessie Luther.' Wilfred was introduced to a strong looking woman with her brown hair neatly piled on top of her head. Her sleeves were pushed up so the cuffs did not interfere with the loom she worked at. Jessie stood up and shook hands with Wilfred.

'This shop is marvellous,' Wilfred enthused. 'You have these patients making some wonderful crafts. Have you taught them all yourself?.'

'Yes. I believe it helps them to heal faster if they have creative things to occupy their time.'

'How would you like to come to Labrador? There are whole villages that would benefit from your teaching. The people there are very poor and need to learn new crafts so that they can support their families, especially those fishermen who have been injured and can no longer fish. Just think how proud they would feel if they could make some of these woodcarvings.'

'That all sounds very nice,' Miss Luther replied, sitting back down at her loom. 'But my work is here. I couldn't possibly go to such a far away place as Labrador.'

But Wilfred was not easily discouraged. He stayed the entire afternoon at the workshop, watching as lovely pots were shaped on the potter's wheel, metal pieces were heated and shaped into interesting designs, wooden animals and birds emerged from blocks of wood, and mats were woven on the looms.

'Marvellous, marvellous,' he kept saying. 'This is just what we need.'

Jessie sighed at Wilfred's insistence and finally said. 'I can't come myself, but if you find me some volunteers I'll train them and then they can go to Labrador.'

It seemed a good compromise, but it did not work out. The two women trained with Miss Luther and went to Labrador, but they did not stay. They quarrelled with each other and then left after a few weeks.

The next year Miss Luther offered to go herself, but only for three months. 'I don't want to leave my work in Boston completely.'

However, Wilfred and the Mission work won Jessie over and by 1907 she had become a permanent member of the staff. She set up craft workshops for the women, older girls and disabled fishermen. The mat industry was the most well known, but the fine workmanship on gloves, moccasins and baskets was popular too. Men made carvings of native animals and birds from ivory, wood and stone. Jessie was kept busy. It was very satisfying work, and she did not even mind the cold weather.

'Are those reindeer I see grazing on the Mission lawn?' one of the summer volunteers asked, when he arrived at St. Anthony in 1909. 'Where did they come from?'

Wilfred's cook laughed.

'Yes, they are all the way from Lapland. The Doctor brought them last autumn. The

Canadian government gave him a grant to pay for them too.'

'But why reindeer? Don't you have caribou here? Why did he need another kind of deer?'

'Well,' she replied, 'there are no cows here. It's too cold and they cost too much to feed. But children need fresh milk. So the Doctor decided that reindeer would be the answer. They feed themselves on the moss that grows everywhere here, they give milk, their meat is good to eat and their hides make good winter clothing.'

Over the years Wilfred tried many things to help his people in Newfoundland and Labrador. Some worked better than others, but his first concern was to improve how the people lived so they could be healthy and earn a good living.

HAPPINESS AND HARDSHIP

'I'm fit as a fiddle,' Wilfred argued with Jessie Luther as he tried to get out of bed. It was 1908 and he had been rescued from the ice pan only a week before. His frostbitten hands and feet were still bound up in bandages and the Mission staff were struggling to keep Wilfred still while he recovered. 'I'm sure I can manage just fine with a walking stick. Now please pass me my clothes.'

'No,' Miss Luther replied firmly. She worried about how much older Wilfred looked since his rescue. The grey streaks in his brown hair and moustache had not been there a week ago, or the lines on his face. 'Dr. Little says you must stay in bed and rest. You have had a terrible ordeal. Remember how you said you wanted to write your story? Why not dictate it to me now? The Mission could publish it in its magazine *Toilers of the Sea.*'

The idea was a good one and Wilfred lay back in the bed while he began to retell the adventure of the ice pan and of the brave fishermen who had rescued him. He paused a while when he remembered his dogs Moody, Watch, and Spy who had to be sacrificed to keep him alive. And once more he thanked God for watching over him.

Wilfred's story *Adrift on an Ice Pan* was soon published and was a huge success. People in Britain, Canada and the United States read it, and Wilfred became famous. When he spoke on his tours crowds of people came to hear him. It was the perfect opportunity to tell even more people about the Mission work, and even more money and volunteers arrived each summer at St. Anthony.

In 1909, after Wilfred had fully recovered, he sailed to England to meet with the Mission Council. He also visited his mother and persuaded her to come to America with him.

'It will be great fun,' Wilfred encouraged her, 'as long as you feel fit enough?'

Mrs. Grenfell smiled. 'I may be seventy-eight,' she replied 'but I can still travel. Why shouldn't I see America before I die? When do we leave?'

Once aboard the ship *Mauretania* something happened that changed Wilfred's life dramatically. His mother spent a great deal of time in their cabin, so Wilfred was free to mingle with other guests. Among them was an elegant young woman dressed in black. Wilfred did not know who she was and no one offered to introduce them. However, he saw her many times over the voyage and began to realize he wanted to marry her! The day before the ship arrived at New York, Wilfred knew he had to take action or he might never see this fascinating person again.

'May I sit down?' Wilfred asked the young woman who was sitting on a deck chair.

'Of course,' she smiled.

Wilfred did not know how to begin, so he burst out with, 'I hope you are not one of those girls who wastes their time with useless society parties.'

The girl was no longer smiling. 'How dare you lecture me. You don't even know my name, much less what I do with my time.'

Startled but not at a loss for words, Wilfred replied, 'Your name does not matter. I am more concerned with your future name, that is if you will marry me.'

'Don't you think you should meet my family first?' the girl shot back, and then, smiling once more, she extended her hand. 'I'm Anne MacClanahan, Dr. Grenfell. I have heard much about you and read your story. Do you really think I would like living in Newfoundland?'

Wilfred needed no more encouragement. He spent the rest of the voyage telling Anne about the Mission and all the work being done there. Anne was soon won over. Even though she was twenty years younger than Wilfred, they fell in love and were married later that year in Chicago, surrounded by her family and friends and Wilfred's mother.

Life in St. Anthony changed when Anne

arrived. The Mission staff built a lovely two storey house for them, and Anne shipped all her furniture and clothing from Chicago. It was quite a performance. The people, who were used to living with just the bare necessities, were amazed at all Anne's fancy tables, chairs and lamps. When Anne gave a birthday lunch for Wilfred at the end of February, all the village came to gawp at the fancy linen and dishes. They wondered if Anne would really be happy in the small village of St. Anthony.

It was a big change for everyone, but Anne soon settled in. Wilfred was quite disorganised. His new wife was the opposite. She became his secretary: answering his letters, editing his manuscripts, organising his speaking tours and keeping Wilfred in line.

Although everyone loved the Doctor, one of his irritating faults was to rush off to do something and forget something else that he had promised to do. Now Anne was there to remind him of those forgotten duties. She also altered his way of dressing.

'You can't wear that,' Anne said, as Wilfred

got ready for the missionary society meeting. 'Bright yellow socks! And that old tweed suit! I thought I took that out of your suitcase. Wear the black one. It's more business like.'

Wilfred was well known for his strange mismatched outfits. He was often too busy thinking about his patients to bother with what he put on. It did not matter so much when he was visiting patients. But on his speaking tours people were often puzzled at his attire.

Wilfred looked down at his socks. They looked fine to him and he liked his tweed suit. 'Are you sure? Oh well then, it won't take a minute to change.' Anne just shook her head.

Anne did not enjoy the outdoors the way her husband did, but she was quite happy to stay in St. Anthony and organise the Mission work there. She shared Wilfred's enthusiasm of working for God by helping the people of Labrador and Newfoundland.

***

'You're a terrible businessman, Dr. Grenfell. You have done a lot of good work for the Mission, but the financial affairs are in a mess.

You have been careless.' Francis Woods spoke with some exasperation. It was 1910 and he had been sent to Newfoundland by the Royal National Mission to Deep Sea Fishermen once again to check on Wilfred's work.

Wilfred was exasperated too. 'Do you know the endless number of things I have to do? I just came in from the sea at 1 a.m. this morning. I have piles of correspondence to see to, reports to read, and more patients to visit. I don't have time for much else. I need an accountant.'

'But you will not listen to one,' Mr. Woods responded. 'I have tried to sort out your affairs and then you make decisions that change all the accounting. Some of the people that you hired made things even worse with their mismanagement.' Mr. Woods tried to speak more softly. 'Dr. Grenfell, I know you are here to serve God. I am not accusing you of any wrong-doing. But you don't understand how to handle money.'

Wilfred knew that Mr. Woods spoke the

truth. 'I am sorry that I entrusted those other people with the money. I thought they were good men and knew about business. But you do see that we need a North American Mission Council, don't you? It is too difficult to manage everything from England.'

'Oh yes, I do know that. You have not listened to us in England for some time. I have come with a proposal from the Council about what should be done.'

It was a difficult time for Wilfred and the Mission. For a number of years Wilfred had been raising money in Canada and the United States for Labrador and Newfoundland without sending any to the Council in England. The Mission Council worried that there would be no money to keep the work in the North Sea and the Irish Sea going. But the people in America who were giving the money did not want it to go to England. They wanted to support Wilfred and the work in Labrador. Things finally had to change in 1912.

Wilfred had to separate himself from the Royal National Mission to Deep Sea Fisherman and form his own mission. It was a tricky business to work out. Everyone, except Wilfred, worried about who would handle the money and do the job well. In the end governors were appointed from all three countries, two from Canada, two from England and two from the United States. Wilfred was to carry on with all his projects and caring for the people, but he had to listen to the Directors from the Board and only spend the money they allowed. Wilfred was also appointed Superintendent and the new Mission was known as the International Grenfell Association.

***

'You are too old to go to war,' Anne protested to her husband. 'You're fifty years old. There are many other doctors who are younger and able to leave their work to go to France. You are needed here with your patients and with your family.'

While Wilfred understood his wife's concern, he would not change his mind.

'I am going to miss you and the boys ... of

course I am ... little Wilfred is almost five and Kinloch is only three. But I must do my part. I am still a British citizen.'

Anne sighed. The two children played at her feet oblivious to the war and to their father's decision to go off and fight. The war had been raging in Europe for a year now and soon Wilfred would be one of the troops Marching off to war - eager to do his bit to help. After joining the Harvard University Medical Unit in 1915, he sailed for France.

As he headed off for yet another adventure he thought over the changes that had taken place in the last year. 'Eleanor Storr volunteered to be an army nurse - that was quite a wrench. She was so good at running the children's home. Then several of the doctors and nurses also signed up. I was concerned about the hiring of new personnel, but it is good that we still have Dr. Little and Dr. Curtis on hand. They both decided to remain to run the hospitals. I am leaving capable people to do the work.'

KNIGHTED IN THE KING'S SERVICE

'Welcome to the front line, Dr. Grenfell. We have lots of work for you to do,' said the army doctor in charge of the hospital. 'We have hundreds of wounded soldiers, all needing attention. Our most important task is to make sure the wounds are cleaned and dressed. The more serious cases need surgery.'

It was January 1916 and Wilfred had arrived in France. It was cold and he was appalled at the numbers of soldiers lined up on stretchers waiting for attention. He began his work immediately.

'This soldier's leg has gone gangrenous,' he said quietly to the nurse. 'It is too late to treat it. I will have to operate and amputate it.' It seemed he said that all too often. If the wounds were left untreated for more than six hours, then they went septic. Even though Wilfred worked as many hours as he could caring for the soldiers, he still took time to think about how to prevent some of the problems.

'Living in those trenches is causing as many medical problems as being shot by the enemy,' Wilfred said to his commander. 'The trenches are full of filth and mud, breeding places for all sorts of bacteria, and the men are getting just as sick from it. Look at the trench-foot problem. It is like frostbite, only worse, because it actually rots the foot on the inside. Our soldiers need better boots to protect them and better conditions too. And we need to treat them faster when they are ill.'

'I know,' his commander replied. 'We are now setting up advanced dressing stations closer to the trenches so the men can be treated as soon as they are wounded. And now the army has given us more ambulances and more doctors and nurses. We are doing all we can. I don't see what I can do about the clothing.'

Well I do,' and with his usual energy for solving problems, Wilfred got to work.

Using what he had learned in Labrador about how to stay dry and warm in bad conditions, Wilfred designed his own uniforms. He sent the designs to the British Medical Journal, where they were published with complete descriptions of the materials and why they were needed. Both the army and the doctors read them with interest.

Wilfred was not able to stay to see his reforms implemented because he had to return to England after three months. The Mission requested he come back to work for them. But he did continue helping the army by writing articles in England about the work of the army doctors.

***

While Wilfred was away other changes occurred at the Mission. Jessie Luther, who was in charge of the craft industries, resigned.

'Mrs. Grenfell, you have interfered with my work and prevented me from selling only the best work,' Jessie complained to Anne.

'That is just the problem,' Anne replied. 'You are so particular that you only allow a few men and women to contribute when so many others want to sell their work too. Why not let them try to sell their crafts, and the buyers can decide? Everyone should have a chance.'

'But if we put inferior crafts in the stores, no one will want to buy anything from Labrador. It will all be considered poor work.'

'Nonsense,' Anne declared.

And so the discussion went on for many months between Miss Luther and Mrs. Grenfell, until one day Jessie wrote a letter to Wilfred saying she could no longer work for the Mission. Wilfred was sad, but he agreed with his wife. He recommended to the Board of Directors of the Mission that they accept Jessie's resignation.

Anne quickly took over Jessie's work. She sorted through all the finished products and bundled them up for shipping to the various shops in St. John's and England. Anne had even contacted some of her friends in the United States and asked them to set up shops in New England, so that the crafts would sell more widely. This helped a great deal because during the war the price of fish dropped and the fishermen made even less money with their catches.

***

'There is a telegram for you, Dr. Grenfell. I think you should read it right away,' said the young man, who was acting as his secretary.

It was the end of 1916 and Wilfred was travelling through Canada, speaking to various groups about the Mission work.

'Is there a problem at the Mission?' Wilfred inquired.

'Yes, and it is about your speech in Montreal. The newspapers reported that you described Newfoundland as a terrible place where the fishermen spend all their time drinking and hurting their families. Some people are really angry at you.'

'But I didn't say any such thing! Send a telegram back saying I don't understand this. I love the people of Labrador and would never speak against them.' Wilfred said.

It turned out that the newspaper had got it wrong, and they printed an apology to Wilfred and the Mission. But it was not enough to stop some of Wilfred's critics from causing more trouble. Some asked the Newfoundland government to investigate the Mission to see if they were making money off the people of Labrador. Reluctantly the Prime Minister sent a commission to interview the fishermen and settlers, look into the cooperative stores' accounts, examine how the hospitals were run and check out the other Mission work.

'Prime Minister, we have found that Dr. Grenfell is completely innocent of the charges,' the spokesman of the commission reported. 'Neither he nor the Mission have made any money and in fact Dr. Grenfell himself has generously given away much of his own money to help the people. We would also like to commend the Mission and its staff for everything they have done so far for our people.'

Wilfred was overjoyed that his critics had been silenced and he praised God for the honest report that had been given. From that time on, there were few who would criticise the Mission's work.

***

'Dr. Grenfell, we have a problem. The Mission work has grown so much that most of our buildings need to be enlarged or at least repaired. One orphanage is overcrowded, a new hospital is needed in North West River, and places like Flower's Cove and Cartwright need new nursing stations. To cover all the expenses we need to raise one and a half millions dollars.'

It was 1920, twenty-eight years since Wilfred had first seen the shores of Newfoundland and Labrador. There were now five hospitals, nine nursing stations and two children's homes serving the communities up and down the coast, and all of them cost money to run. Donations to the Mission had been down during the war and still were not back to their usual level. If money was not found soon some buildings would have to be closed.

'Then I guess I'll have to get busy,' Wilfred said.

'Yes, but we think you need to do your fund-raising full-time,' one of the directors said.

'And leave the work here? How could I do that?'

'I know it is a sacrifice for you, but it is for the good of the Mission. There are plenty of good men and women to carry on the work if we can get the money we need. Yes, we need to pray and ask God to help, but we need to let Americans, Canadians and British people know about the needs. You are the only one who can do that. You can tell them first hand what it is like here, who the people of Labrador are, and what the Mission needs to do God's work.'

Wilfred knew it was the right thing to do, so he reluctantly said good-bye to his friends and co-workers, packed up his family and moved to Boston. His wife was pleased. Their two boys were now old enough for school and she could have them educated in her home country. They now had a young daughter too. Her name was Rosamund and we would be ready for school in a few years time. As far as Anne was concerned this was a very timely decision. But Wilfred had not left Labrador for good. He would be back often, still sailing up and down in the summer, visiting patients and old friends.

Meanwhile, he had money to raise. Wilfred travelled tirelessly. People flocked to hear him. His autobiography *Labrador Doctor* had just been published. Many had read it and wanted to know more.

'My heart is heavy for the people of Labrador,' he began his talk. 'Imagine you are with me on my last call one evening to a thirty-four year old woman who has two naked children. All they have eaten that winter is white flour and molasses. She doesn't complain, even though she is plagued with a terrible cough and chest pains. Her children are so weak from malnutrition that they cannot play as others do. They just sit in their cabin, slowly dying. Surely your heart aches for them?

'Or come with me to an old fisherman's hut I know. He can no longer fish the seas, so he cuts timber for ships' boilers. When I visited him last he did not even have a warm garment for the winter. I had nothing to give him except my own suit, which I gladly parted with. He was both embarrassed and grateful. These are the people God has sent us to help and, by his grace, we have been able to do a great deal. But the work cannot stop because the people's needs do not stop. There is always another family starving or sick with disease. Your help means they will have food and a doctor to care for them, and most important of all a chance to hear the good news of Jesus Christ.'

Many hearts were moved by Wilfred's appeals and within the first year of his speaking tour half a million dollars was raised. The Mission workers praised God for supplying the money and were thankful for Wilfred's gift of speaking.

***

In 1927 a new hospital was built in St.

Anthony. Enough money had been raised to build a handsome brick building, with all the latest equipment. It was classed with the best hospitals in North America at the time.

'Are you sure you should go up the coast just now?' Anne asked, as Wilfred was preparing to sail north on the *Strathcona II*. 'Sir William and Lady Allardyce are being sent by King George himself to open the new hospital. Will you be back in time? You can't miss this ceremony.'

'Don't worry,' Wilfred reassured her. 'I will return in plenty of time. I don't want to miss it either.' He kissed his wife goodbye and bounded off to the ship.

It looked like Wilfred would keep his promise. The waters were smooth and the *Strathcona II* made good time. Wilfred called in at settlements, treating patients and visiting some old friends. But on the way back a small fishing trawler caught up with the steam ship.

'Doctor, please turn back. My wife has taken ill suddenly and I don't know what to do,' the fisherman pleaded.

Wilfred did not hesitate. 'The sea is smooth. I am sure we can be there and back in no time,' he reassured his crew.

So the *Strathcona II* turned north once more and followed the fisherman to his settlement. Once there, Wilfred cared for the woman as best he could. However, the return trip was not smooth. Fog set in and the ship, going full speed, went off course.

'Doctor, look ahead!' came the cry, just as the ship ran up on to some rocks. Everyone was thrown to the floor with the sudden stop. The ship was stranded, listing to one side and being pounded by the waves on the other.

'What do we do now?'

'Get out the life boats. We have to abandon the ship. Let us pray we can all get out safely.'

Wilfred sat with the other crew and passengers, and watched the *Strathcona II* as she tipped more and more to one side. It just seemed like a matter of time before she would slip off the rocks and sink. Miraculously she did slip off, but remained afloat!

'Praise God,' Wilfred shouted. 'He has saved our ship. Let's see if she is seaworthy.'

The crew could hardly believe the mess they found aboard. Every piece of furniture and all the fittings had been smashed by the impact. The pumps were clogged, so everyone grabbed a bucket and began to bail out the water.

'Let's see if we can raise some steam.' Wilfred called out from the boiler. He began shovelling coal in, coaxing the boiler to heat. Others came to help, and soon the boiler was glowing hot. 'She may not look too healthy, but I think this old ship will get us home. We may even make it in time for the ceremony.'

Listing heavily, the *Strathcona II* limped into St. Anthony harbour just in time for Wilfred to change into his good clothes and join the ceremony. The entire town was there, along with the Governor of Newfoundland and Labrador. All the ships in the harbour had their flags flying and there was a guard of honour of the Church Boys' Brigade, and the Mission Boy Scouts and Girl Guides.

'I open the hospital of St. Anthony in the name of his Majesty King George.' Sir William Allardyce announced, and then he went on. 'I am also pleased to announce that his Majesty has graciously conferred the honour of Knight Commander of St. Michael and St. George on Dr. Grenfell. He will now be known as Sir Wilfred Grenfell.'

A great cheer went up from the crowd and both Wilfred and his wife smiled and waved.

A year later Wilfred and Anne went to Buckingham Palace to receive the medal from the King himself.

'This is such a wonderful honour, dear,' Anne said later that day. 'Just think, Sir Wilfred and Lady Anne Grenfell.'

Wilfred smiled as he sat holding the medal. 'I don't think my father would believe this, if he knew.' Then he looked at Anne. 'But it is not the best honour. Serving the King of heaven is better, and receiving his 'well done' means more than all the medals anyone can receive.'

THE ONLY REAL
ADVENTURE OF LIFE

'You have to start to take it easy, Dr. Grenfell.' Wilfred's doctor was lecturing him about his health - but he wasn't too sure if his patient was listening. 'As your doctor I must warn you that another heart attack like this one will kill you. You must retire.'

'Retire from God's work? That's impossible.' Wilfred started to get up from his chair in the doctor's office. Then he sat down again. 'I'm not afraid of death, not since my experience many years ago on the ice pan. Death is really the greatest advance in life. I have much to look forward to in heaven. Until then, I will work to serve my Lord.'

'I understand your love for God and his work. I will have to report your health to the

Mission since I am a member of the Board. However, I think we can work something out that both your wife and I can agree on. She is very worried about you.'

It was 1929 and Wilfred had had two heart attacks. They slowed him down a little, but only until he felt well enough to travel again. Anne did get him to agree to limit his travels to a few large cities, where bigger crowds of people could hear him. She also suggested he give some of his talks and lectures on the radio. That way Wilfred could still reach people in smaller towns. He also spent time writing his books, with Anne's help. Together they wrote a new edition of his autobiography and called it *Forty Years for Labrador*.

At the end of 1930 a worldwide depression caused problems. Over the years the government had tried to do its best to help the people of Newfoundland and Labrador by building roads and docks in St. John's and even a new railroad. But all the money had run out by 1931 and the government was in trouble. Wilfred, along with others, was called in to give advice about what should be done.

'The newspapers say you should be the next Governor of Newfoundland, Dr. Grenfell,' said George Whitely, an old friend. 'Would you like the job?'

'Nonsense,' Wilfred replied. 'I'm too old. But I do have some ideas about what to do and I will talk to Lord Amulree, the Commissioner that the British government has sent. He needs to know how much the people in the north of Labrador still need help and not to leave them out of any changes in government plans.'

Wilfred did attend meetings with Lord Amulree and was pleased with the decision made in 1934 to bring in a new government with three Newfoundlanders and three British officials. The Mission was not forgotten, and the new government promised to support the work if the Mission would continue to help the people. It was a good agreement.

***

'This will be my last voyage, I promise,' Wilfred said to Anne in 1932. 'It is such an exciting opportunity. Last year when I went to help chart the coast line, we accomplished a great deal. The Geographical Society has offered to produce charts from our information. This year the *HMS Challenger*, a Royal Naval survey ship, is going to finish the mapping. It's just what Labrador needs. It will open up the coastline and people will be able to open hotels and restaurants, and conduct tours for tourists. It will give them more ways to earn money for their families.' He paused and added with sadness in his voice, ' I'm going to miss them. So many good friends to sit and talk with, or go hunting and fishing with. There are so many yet to hear of God's love. I need to say goodbye to them, Anne.'

'I know you do. Just be careful and listen to your doctor. I told him to make sure you do not overdo it.' And she kissed him goodbye.

Wilfred made that voyage, but not without difficulty. He had several more small heart attacks, and complained vigorously when his doctor told him to slow down. Many old friends turned out to say goodbye. They knew the Mission would continue with good people, but there was no-one like 'the Doctor.'

'Doctor, there are some people I would like you to meet,' said Minnie Pike, Director of the Industrial Department of the Mission.

'Who would that be?' Wilfred was visiting Red Bay for the last time, as part of his voyage.

'Remember the two little blind girls you brought to the children's home years ago?' Minnie motioned for the good looking young women standing behind her to come forward. 'Here are Joan and Mary. They have grown up and are now working here with us. I thought you would like to meet them again.'

Wilfred could not stop grinning. He shook their hands vigorously. 'This is wonderful. How good God has been.'

'Yes, Doctor. God has been good to us,' Mary replied, 'and so have you. Thank you for giving us a good home and an education. Now we want to work for the Mission.'

As Wilfred toured he met other children he had rescued. Now grown up they had returned to work for the Mission as carpenters, engineers, teachers, and hospital workers.

Wilfred's heart was full with thanksgiving.

***

'I must resign, I think,' Wilfred said to Anne sadly, as they sat in their retirement home in Vermont. It was now 1937 and both Wilfred and Anne were in very poor health. 'The Mission must go on without me.'

Anne squeezed his hand. 'I know it is the right thing to do. Although I'm sure they will still want to hear your ideas and suggestions. It is just time to let others do the work.' Anne winced with pain.

'You need to rest, my dear,' Wilfred told his wife, and he helped her to her bed.

But Anne was as stubborn as Wilfred and would not stay still as the doctors ordered. She still read each letter that came and answered it. She also wrote to friends, encouraging them to continue to help the Mission. She helped organise fund-raising events and opened more shops to sell the handicrafts made in Labrador.

The following year, the doctors decided that Anne needed another operation. A tumour had grown in her abdomen. So Anne and Wilfred travelled to Boston and lived in a hotel there.

'I'm sure Anne will be better after the operation on Wednesday,' Wilfred muttered to himself. 'Then we can get back to working for the Mission.'

But others weren't so sure and after Anne came out from surgery people began to realise how ill she really was. The surgery had not helped. Anne died a few weeks later. Wilfred surprised everyone with his calm acceptance. 'She is in heaven now, with no more pain. And one day soon I will see her again.'

***

In the summer of 1939 Wilfred made his last visit to Newfoundland and Labrador.

'Do not excite him too much,' was the medical advice given to the people of St. Anthony. 'We are all eager to see him, but his heart is not strong.'

So the welcome was subdued but full of love for the man they all admired. A triumphal arch of evergreen boughs was erected at the harbour and the entire town was on shore when he stepped out of the steamer. After resting, Wilfred was taken on a tour of the hospital that now housed two hundred patients and treated one hundred out patients. The disabled fishermen proudly showed the carvings they made to sell in the shops.

'This is a most uplifting and inspiring occasion,' Wilfred said at the end of it all.

After resting for several days, Wilfred then sailed north to Cartwright, where he was taken on a tour of another hospital. Some people who came to meet Wilfred were too young to know all the work he had done, but their parents and even grandparents had told them the stories of the Doctor's many exploits, kindnesses and the gospel he preached.

'I read your essay last night, 'What Christ Means to Me',' an old friend said.

Wilfred nodded. It was an essay that he had written in 1927. It was good to realise that people were still reading and learning from it. This morning had been a good opportunity to sketch the village of St. Anthony from the verandah of the house. The page in front of him showed the rough outline of the harbour and some fishing vessels heading into port.

Wilfred's friend continued to discuss the essay. 'I especially liked the part where you quoted the verse from Psalm 143 that says 'Cause me to know the way wherein I should walk,' as your guide for life. And you go on to say how we should live our lives like Christ did. When he was a carpenter he made his doors and windows so that they did not jam or misfit. And it is just the same for you. You wanted to do your surgery as Christ himself would do it.'

'The only hope of salvation in this world is in Christ, my friend.' Wilfred replied. 'There are many things in the Bible I do not understand. I don't know how Jesus walked on the water or raised the dead. I will understand all of that in heaven. But I do know that our Lord has set the highest possible standard in himself and challenges us to look to him and follow him. With his help I have tried to do just that. I wish I could have done more, but God has only given each of us so much time here on earth. How much I want to hear him say 'Well done, good and faithful servant.' Christ gave his life for me. How could I give anything less.'

Wilfred sailed home again and for a time his health seemed to improve. He managed to lecture a few more times and attend a dinner in New York. Two hundred and fifty workers and volunteers of the Mission attended this dinner to see 'The Doctor.'

Several months later, in October 1940, Wilfred retired to his Vermont home. His children gathered round to see him. Not one to sit still, Wilfred played a game of croquet the day he died. While he had his afternoon rest he went to his heavenly home.

At Wilfred's memorial service in St. Anthony, several portions of Scripture were read. First the Good Samaritan parable and then the parable of the sheep and goats from Matthew 25. Finally 2 Timothy 4:7-8 was read to sum up the life of Sir Wilfred Grenfell.

'I have fought a good fight, I have finished my course, I have kept the faith: Henceforth there is laid up for me a crown of righteousness, which the Lord the righteous judge, shall give me at that day: and not me only, but unto all them also that love his appearing.'

Author Profile

Linda Finlayson is a Canadian living in the Philadelphia area of the United States.

Books, children and an interest in history have all been part of her life for many years. She teaches in Sunday school and in children's clubs, and loves to read about people in history. Linda's husband is the Library Director at Westminster Theological Seminary, and they have a teenage son. They attend Gwynedd Valley Orthodox Presbyterian Church.

Personal Thoughts on Wilfred Grenfell
by Linda Finlayson

When I was in school I had to give a speech about an exciting person. My father suggested Dr. Grenfell, and gave me *Adrift on an Ice Pan* to read. I was hooked. I wanted to know more!

Many think being a Christian is boring because you have to obey all of God's laws. But they are wrong because obeying God and listening to him is really a very great adventure. Wilfred Grenfell served God as a missionary doctor and travelled over two continents, crossed the Atlantic many times, drove a dogsled. and was knighted by the King. Yet, he never forgot to tell people the gospel.

Wilfred reminds me of some boys I know. They have lots of energy and long for an exciting life. They don't like school much, but are gifted in many ways. Wilfred was good at athletics, loved sailing, and was a good storyteller and he used those gifts to be a missionary. Without his energy and stamina he could not have withstood the rugged and dangerous conditions. Wilfred did everything he could to help and heal the people of Labrador and Newfoundland. Most importantly he shared the gospel with them. The International Grenfell Association is still doing the work he began.

I wanted to write Wilfred's story because I want to encourage boys and girls to use their gifts to serve God. Serving God is always an adventure.

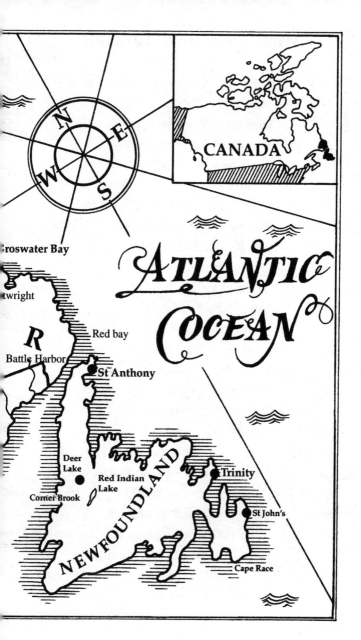

Wilfred Grenfell Timeline

1865	Wilfred Grenfell born, February 28.
	Rudyard Kipling born (author)
	Disinfectant invented.
	President Lincoln assassinated.
1866	Transatlantic cable completed.
	Beatrix Potter born (author).
	Butch Cassidy born (criminal).
1867	Diamonds discovered in South Africa.
	Alaska purchased from Russia
	Dynamite invented.
	Marie Curie born (scientist).
1869	Suez Canal opened.
	Mahatma Gandhi born (politician).
1870	Vladmir Ilyich Lenin born (politician).
1871	Great fire destroys Chicago.
1873	Colour photographs invented.
1876	Telephone invented.
1879	Electric light bulb invented.
1882	Wilfred Grenfell moves to London.
1884	Development of first motorcycle.
1885	Development of first car.
1888	Wilfred Grenfell graduates.
1892	Wilfred Grenfell makes his first trip to Newfoundland and Labrador.
1893	New Zealand gives women the vote.
1898	C.S.Lewis born.

1900	Boxer Rebellion in China.
1901	Oil discovered in Texas, U.S.A.
	First British submarine launched.
	Commonwealth of Australia founded.
1903	Development of first aircraft.
1907	Plastic invented.
1909	North Pole reached.
	Wilfred Grenfell marries.
1911	The South Pole reached.
1912	The Titanic sinks.
1914-1918	The First World War.
1920	U.S.A gives women the vote.
1927	Wilfred Grenfell is honoured with a Knighthood for his work on the Labrador coast.
	First transatlantic solo flight.
1928	Penicillin discovered.
	Television invented.
1930	Pluto discovered
1938	Wilfred Grenfell's wife dies.
1939	Digital computer invented.
1940	Wilfred Grenfell dies.

Quiz

1. What were the names of the dogs that Wilfred Grenfell had to kill on the ice pack?

2. What bit of the body did Wilfred Grenfell see in a jar in Dr. Russell's study?

3. What Evangelist did Wilfred Grenfell listen to one day which made him turn to God?

4. What did Wilfred Grenfell use on the ship to keep his patients steady?

5. Which Newfoundland town was on fire when Wilfred Grenfell arrived?

6. What is a Komatik?

7. How did Wilfred encourage the women in Labrador to make money for their families?

8. Who did Wilfred meet on board the Mauretania on his way to the U.S.A.?

9. What honour did Wilfred Grenfell receive from King George?

10. What was the title of the Essay that Wilfred wrote? Would you be able to write something on that subject?

Answers on page 135

Wilfred Grenfell Summary

Who was he?
Wilfred Grenfell was born in 1865 in Parkgate Wales. After a start as a rather poor student he was directed towards medical training by a family friend and doctor, Dr Russell. Though still preferring an active life, medicine was an interesting and fulfilling career choice for him.

What was his work?
Wilfred was converted after listening to the evangelist D.L.Moody and was soon working for the Royal National Mission to Deep Sea Fishermen. After his initial work with the fishing vessels in the North Sea Wilfred became heavily involved with the settlements and towns along the coast of Newfoundland and Labrador. On arrival in Labrador in 1892 his immediate task was to provide a system of medical care for migratory fishermen. But Grenfell accomplished much more than that with hospitals, schools and local businesses all part of his far reaching vision.

What about his adventures?
He had many adventures on sea and on the land. One of the most notorious being his narrow escape on the ice pack, during which he had to kill three of his dogs in order to survive.

Quiz Answers
1. Moody, Watch and Spy; 2. A brain; 3. D L Moody; 4 Heavy barrels; 5. St. John's; 6. A Sledge; 7. By helping them make and sell their crafts; 8. Anne MacClanahan - his future wife; 9. A Knighthood; 10. What Christ means to me.

Newfoundland Geography

Newfoundland and Labrador would rank fourth in size behind Alaska, Texas and California ... if it were one of the United States. It is almost one-and-three-quarters times the size of Great Britain.

Land Area
Newfoundland - 111,390 km2. Labrador - 294,330 km2. Total area: 405,720 km².

Water Area
34,030 km². Newfoundland Coast - 9,656 km. Labrador Coast - 7,886 km Total - 17,542 km

Population
St. John's is the capital of Newfoundland and Labrador. Its population is 99,182. The population of Labrador is 27,864 but there are 600,000 caribou (a type of reindeer). The population of the whole province is 512,930.

Time Zones
Newfoundland is located in a time zone unique in North America, half an hour later than Atlantic Time, one and a half hours later than Central Canada and four and a half hours later than the west coast of the country. Depending on what part of Labrador you are in you could either be on Atlantic Time or Newfoundland time.

Newfoundland Symbols

Newfoundland Motto
The translation of the motto is 'Seek ye first the Kingdom of God.'

Official Bird
The Atlantic Puffin..

Newfoundland Dogs
These are large dogs with great size and strength. A heavy coat protects them from the icy waters of Newfoundland. Their feet are large, strong, and webbed so they may travel easily over marshes and shores. A Newfoundland must be a large dog with powerful hindquarters and a lung capacity which enables him to swim for great distances.

Floral Emblem
The Pitcher Plant is wine and green in colour and can be found on bogs and marshes in Newfoundland and Labrador.

Official Tree
The Black Spruce. This is the favoured tree in the pulp and paper industry and is widely used for lumber, building and firewood. It is extremely hardy and flourishes in Newfoundland's short growing season.

Newfoundland History

The Vikings

In 986 AD Bjarni Herjólsson from Scandinavia sailed along the coast of Newfoundland. Lief Ericson, sailed to North America in the 10th century and named the area Vinland because of the grapes growing there.

The Native Population

When Europeans began explorations Nomadic people from the Subarctic already lived in Newfoundland and Labrador. They shared the land with the Inuit, the Naskapi and Montagnais Natives. Explorers also discovered the Beothuk people. The Micmac who had migrated to from Nova Scotia also lived in the area.

The Europeans

Near the end of the 15th century, Europeans began to search for a Northwest route to Asia and repeatedly visited Newfoundland. In 1497 John Cabot sailed from England and reported that Newfoundland codfish were so thick that he could scoop them up in baskets from the sides of the ship. Fishermen from Europe flocked to the area to take advantage of this plenty.

John Guy, a merchant, brought 39 settlers in 1610. France realized the importance of Newfoundland as a gateway to Canada. St. Johns was burned by French troops in 1696 and fell to the French in 1708. But in 1713 the French were defeated and Newfoundland was returned to the English.

Expansion and Settlement

Labrador was reunited with Newfoundland in 1809 after being claimed by Quebec in 1774. This meant an access to an abundance of wildlife. The seal and fur trades were extremely profitable. The Hudson's Bay Company was established in the area and mass migration from Europe meant that the fishery and seal hunting trade expanded. As the 20th century dawned the fishery was enjoying high world prices and copper was being mined. However a fire destroyed most of St. John's in 1892.

Second World War

The Great Depression wiped out demand for Newfoundland's products. The onset of World War 2 improved Newfoundland's economy however. Newfoundland's location was important for American and Canadian naval and air bases. At the end of the war Newfoundland voted to become Canada's tenth province on March 31, 1949.

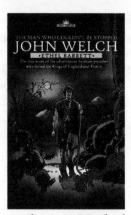

John Welch

The Man Who Couldn't Be Stopped
Ethel Barrett

When he was a boy John was independent, stubborn and had a mind of his own. He ran away and fell in with a gang of thieves. But then he met God. John left his sinful life and became a preacher and with God beside him there was nothing and no one who could stand in his way – not even the King of England or the King of France!

This is the true story of one of Scotland's most adventurous preachers.

As the son-in-law of another fiery Scot – John Knox – John Welch was bound to cause a stir – and he did! Find out about how he conquered roughians, saved a town from the dreaded plague and even dodged a cannon ball!

Extra Features include: Maps, Quiz, Time Line, What was life like then? And Fact Summaries.

ISBN 1 85792 928 4

Trailblazers

Corrie ten Boom, ISBN 1 85792 116X
Joni Eareckson Tada, ISBN 1 85792 833 4
Adoniram Judson, ISBN 1 85792 6609
Isobel Kuhn, ISBN 1 85792 6102
C.S. Lewis, ISBN 1 85792 4878
Martyn Lloyd-Jones,
ISBN 1 85792 3499
George Müller, ISBN 1 85792 5491
John Newton, ISBN 1 85792 834 2
John Paton, ISBN 1 85792 852 0
Mary Slessor, ISBN 1 85792 3480
Hudson Taylor, ISBN 1 85792 4231
William Wilberforce, ISBN 1 85792 3715
Richard Wurmbrand, ISBN 1 85792 2980
Gladys Aylward, ISBN 1 85792 5947

LIGHT KEEPERS

Start collecting this series now!

Ten girls who
changed the world
Corrie Ten Boom, Mary Slessor, Joni Eareckson
Tada, Isobel Kuhn, Amy Carmichael,
Elizabeth Fry, Evelyn Brand, Gladys Aylward,
Catherine Booth, Jackie Pullinger

Ten girls who
made a difference
Monica of Thagaste
Catherine Luther, Susanna Wesley,
Ann Judson, Maria Taylor,
Susannah Spurgeon, Bethan Lloyd-Jones,
Edith Schaeffer, Sabina Wurmbrand,
Ruth Bell Graham.

Ten girls who
made history
Ida Scudder, Betty Green, Jeanette Li,
Mary Jane Kinnaird, Bessie Adams, Emma Dryer,
Lottie Moon, Florence Nightingale,
Henrietta Mears,
Elisabeth Elliot.

LIGHT KEEPERS

Start collecting this series now!

Ten boys who
changed the world
David Livingstone, Billy Graham,
Brother Andrew, John Newton, William Carey,
George Müller, Nicky Cruz,
Eric Liddell, Luis Palau, Adoniram Judson.

Ten boys who
made a difference
Augustine of Hippo,
Jan Hus, Martin Luther,
Ulrich Zwingli, William Tyndale,
Hugh Latimer, John Calvin,
John Knox, Lord Shaftesbury,
Thomas Chalmers.

Ten boys who
made history
Charles Spurgeon, Jonathan Edwards,
Samuel Rutherford, D L Moody,
Martin Lloyd Jones, A W Tozer, John Owen,
Robert Murray McCheyne, Billy Sunday,
George Whitfield.

CHRISTIAN FOCUS

Staying faithful - Reaching out!

Christian Focus Publications publishes books for adults and children under its three main imprints: Christian Focus, Mentor and Christian Heritage. Our books reflect that God's word is reliable and Jesus is the way to know him, and live for ever with him.

Our children's publication list includes a Sunday school curriculum that covers pre-school to early teens; puzzle and activity books. We also publish personal and family devotional titles, biographies and inspirational stories that children will love.

If you are looking for quality Bible teaching for children then we have an excellent range of Bible story and age specific theological books.

From pre-school to teenage fiction, we have it covered!

Find us at our web page:
www.christianfocus.com